# LAKE DISTRICT WA.

## Western Area

Warne Gerrard Guides for Walkers

# LAKE DISTRICT
## WALKS FOR MOTORISTS
## WESTERN AREA

John Parker

**30 sketch maps by the author**

FREDERICK WARNE

FREDERICK WARNE
Penguin Books Ltd, Harmondsworth, Middlesex, England
Viking Penguin Inc., 40 West 23rd Street, New York, New York 10010, U.S.A.
Penguin Books Australia Ltd, Ringwood, Victoria, Australia
Penguin Books Canada Ltd, 2801 John Street, Markham, Ontario, Canada L3R 1B4
Penguin Books (N.Z.) Ltd, 182–190 Wairau Road, Auckland 10, New Zealand

First published 1973
First revised edition 1978
Second revised edition 1979
Third revised edition 1981
Reprinted 1986

The photograph on the front cover shows walkers at the head of Buttermere
and was taken by Tom Parker.

## Publishers' Note

While every care has been taken in the compilation of this book, the
publishers cannot accept responsibility for any inaccuracies. But things
change: paths are sometimes diverted; concrete bridges replace wooden
ones; stiles disappear. Please inform the publishers if you discover
anything like this on your way.

The length of each walk in this book is given in miles and kilometres,
but within the text Imperial measurements are quoted. It is useful to bear
the following approximations in mind: 5 miles = 8 kilometres, ½ mile =
805 metres, 1 metre = 39.4 inches.

Printed and bound in Great Britain by
Cox & Wyman Ltd, Reading

# Contents

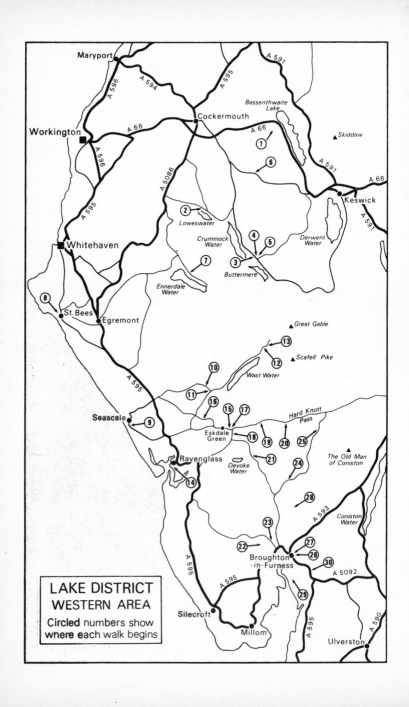

LAKE DISTRICT
WESTERN AREA

Circled numbers show
where each walk begins

# INTRODUCTION

This book is for motorists who are not always slaves to their cars, who wish to sample the joys of the Lake District National Park's superb countryside denied to those who are prisoners of their mobile steel boxes. These walks use the car as the base. Most guides in the past have been of little use to the motorist because they described walks from 'A' to 'B'. All the walks in *this* book are circular — from 'A' to 'A' — 'A' being the walker's car.

Like previous volumes, this guide is not for athletes. It is for those who like a moderate walk with exceptional attractions. It is for photographers, amateur naturalists and easy ramblers who want to savour the natural beauty to the full without enduring a route-march. The walks can be enjoyed by all ages, and by family parties.

This guide is not for fell walkers either. Fine fell guides are already obtainable. It is assumed that there are very many walkers who have no urge to meet the challenge of the wild high places. Mountain accident statistics for the area prove that too many walkers find themselves on the fells without the right equipment to face the rough ground, the strong winds, and the sudden savage storms. From the valleys the fell paths can be seen easily and can offer a dangerous attraction. On the other hand the very delightful valley walks, the lake-shore paths, and the ways to the viewpoints, are not so apparent. They start at farm gates; hide up private-looking drives and behind inns and churchyards. Yet they are rights of way for all to enjoy. This guide explains where some of the best can be found.

I am a fanatical fell walker. But I also love the lush green valleys of the Lake District more than can be expressed. Most fell walkers do not know what they are missing in the valleys. The valleys offer far more variety of scenery and some of the finest views. There is much more to see of Nature. There are hundreds of miles of lower-level paths hardly discovered by modern generations and few of them are shown in current guides to the Lake District. This book is an attempt to introduce more country-goers to the joys that they can offer.

The book has not been written from an armchair. To write this slim volume I have had to walk some 200 miles, and the walks described are the best 30 of those I walked. If some wonder why their favourite walk has been left out it should be remembered that thought had to be given to car parking facilities and the need to provide routes suitable for all ages.

The western and southern areas of the National Park, being

7

more remote, are ideal for those who want to get away from crowds. However, some of the walks are rather longer, and sometimes rougher going, than those shown in the Central and Northern guides. Where this is so ample warning is given. They just require longer time to walk; but none of the walks are for people in a hurry.

## Rights of Way
All the walks described here are on official rights of way, or permissive footpaths, or on public access areas. Some guides have caused trouble and distress to landowners and farmers, as they have encouraged trespass, and indirectly been the cause of damage to walls and fences. This guide describes officially designated paths and bridleways, the right of passage over which cannot be properly challenged. There is the proviso, however, that routes are legally changed from time to time, in which case the altered alignment should be signposted.

The rights are plain. The responsibilities should be recognised too. Right of passage across a farm field, for instance, does not mean a right to wander off the path to picnic. Grass is an important growing crop which can be damaged by trampling. Dogs need to be kept under proper control. It is strongly recommended that every dog should be on a lead when passing through farmland. Even 'harmless' dogs, if they are boisterous and playful among farm stock, can cause damage.

Farmers have a right to put an unlocked gate across a right of way. Walkers have a responsibility, after opening such a gate, to close it after them to prevent stock wandering. Litter — even sweet wrappings — should be taken back to the car.

## Equipment
A map is not strictly necessary if this guide is carried, as the routes are described in detail and sketch maps provided. All one needs to know is one's left hand from one's right. A 1:50,000 Ordnance Survey map, however, adds interest and helps to identify points in distant prospects that are not mentioned. Such a map is also the best to show the local roads. A pocket-compass is not necessary either, but can add interest.

The most important item of equipment is footwear but the comparatively expensive fell-walking boots are not needed here. Footwear should above all be well-fitting and reasonably waterproof. Ideally, to prevent blistering, boots should be worn over woollen socks. Completely smooth soles can be a misery, as they slide on wet stones and grass and waste energy.

Clothing should be comfortable, and lightweight waterproofs should be carried.

Even if the intention is to be back at the car for a meal, some food should be carried in case you are delayed. It can save misery!

8

Other optional equipment could include cameras, sketch pads, plant or bird identification books and binoculars.

The best equipment of all is an eye to see everything afresh.

## The Lake District National Park and The National Trust

The whole of the Lake District, from the A6 in the east to the coast of Cumberland in the west is Britain's largest National Park, an area of 866 square miles. This does not mean that the whole of this land belongs to the nation and that you can wander on it at will. It means that it is a very specially protected area where any unsightly development is prevented. Its governing body — the National Park Planning Board — also has a duty to help the public to enjoy the amenities. It can, for instance, acquire land for public access and for car parks. It provides an information service, and the information centres can be found in some of the busier areas. Brockhole, the National Park Visitor Centre, is a house set among lovely gardens by the lake shore between Windermere and Ambleside. There is a permanent exhibition there and lectures and filmshows illustrating all that the Lake District National Park has to offer are presented. The Centre is well worth a visit.

The National Park also has a ranger service. There are several professional rangers and a lot of weekend volunteers. They could be met on the footpaths and access areas described here and can be recognised by their armbands and badges. They are there to encourage good behaviour, to enforce by-laws and the litter act, but their main function is to be friendly and helpful. They are 'mobile information centres'.

The National Trust, on the other hand, in spite of what its title might suggest, has nothing to do with government. It is a private body entirely supported by voluntary contributions. It exists to acquire land and property of natural beauty and of historic importance, for its protection and for the public to enjoy. By great good fortune the National Trust is one of the largest landowners in the Lake District National Park. It owns fells, lakes and valleys, and protects them for all time. Many farms are in National Trust ownership, too. The Trust also has some information points in various parts of the Lake District.

The National Park Planning Board and the National Trust operate together in the Lake District for the public good.

## The Country Code

Your walks can be marred if you cause trouble to farmers, land-owners and fellow walkers but unpleasant encounters can be avoided given a little common sense and imagination. Some of the following points have been mentioned already but they are so important that they are repeated.

Litter is offensive and dangerous and should never be left. Children, and the elderly, are apt to be forgetful and they should be reminded of this.

Dogs, even normally harmless friendly dogs, should be properly controlled. A lead should be carried and used where necessary.

If closed gates are encountered they should be closed after you.

The other points of the country code are a matter of common sense, too. Keep to the paths. Avoid damaging drystone walls. Beware against contaminating drinking water. Respect other people's property, privacy and right to enjoy peace and quiet. Guard against risk of fire—especially in or near woodland or open heath. Resist the temptation to uproot or damage plants, ferns, shrubs and trees.

Last, but not least, drive carefully and walk carefully on the narrow country roads.

## Useful addresses

If a right of way is obstructed, it would be of service if the matter were reported, with precise details and location, as soon as possible. Footpaths are the responsibility of the National Park authority. Complaints should be sent to the National Park Officer, Lake District Special Planning Board, Busher Walk, Kendal, Cumbria.

Accommodation and tourist information: Cumbria Tourist Board, Ellerthwaite, Windermere, Cumbria.

National Park Information Service: Bank House, High Street, Windermere, Cumbria.

The National Trust: Broadlands, Borrans Road, Ambleside, Cumbria.

The National Park Visitor Centre: Brockhole, Windermere.

The Friends of the Lake District is the local preservation society: The Secretary, Gowan Knott, Kendal Road, Staveley, Kendal.

Cumbria Naturalists' Trust concerns itself with the local preservation of nature and owns several reserves: The Secretary, Rydal Road, Ambleside, Cumbria.

4¼ miles [7 km]

O.S. 1:50,000 Sheet No. 89 or 90

---

This is a superb 'away from it all' walk only marred at one or two points by the sound of distant traffic speeding on the A66. But there is hardly anything to match the utter peacefulness by the ruin of the old church, or the magnificence of the lofty views over Bassenthwaite Lake to the Skiddaws. This walk is for those who wish to shed worldly cares. It is best done when the weather is fair and the views clear, and it should be savoured slowly like a glass of old wine. There are sheep pastures where dogs should be on leads.

What better place to start a walk than a famed hostelry? In this case it is the Pheasant Inn at the foot of Bassenthwaite Lake. This is on a loop of old road just off the A66. Driving towards Cockermouth from Keswick it is about seven miles. From Cockermouth it is about five miles. The inn is fronted by a section of old road on which one can park.

Walk up the road signposted 'Wythop Mill' (pronounced 'withop'), alongside the Pheasant Inn. Ignore the road into the forest and go on up the hill. Well on up the road is a peculiar piece of yew topiary looking rather like a monster on a plinth. There is a view back to Bassenthwaite. The little hamlet approached is Routenbeck. Near the brow of the hill ignore track on right labelled 'The Riggs', and beyond it find a seat on the left for the weary to rest under an old larch tree. Just beyond this seat turn left as signed 'Public Footpath Kelswick'. This is through a kissing-gate by an old iron sign which says 'Public Footpath 1911'. The path is a green one and soon there is another seat on the right of the path; below and beyond it can be seen Wythop Church. There is a view over the foot of Bassenthwaite with the northern foothills of Skiddaw. The hill on the left is Binsey, often used by hang-gliders. Continue on up to gate. Go through it and close it afterwards unless it has obviously been propped open by the farmer. After a short distance a track is joined. Go along it right. The pleasant green track rises only gradually.

As the brow of the hill is reached there are views over the plains around Cockermouth to the sea. If the weather is clear it is possible to see north-westwards over the Solway to the Scottish Criffell. The track descends alongside drystone wall for a time then goes off to the left to leave it. There is a glimpse of a fell ahead, Clough Head, the northern tip of the Helvellyn range. The flash of white in the quarry above the track is a vein of quartz. There is a view down

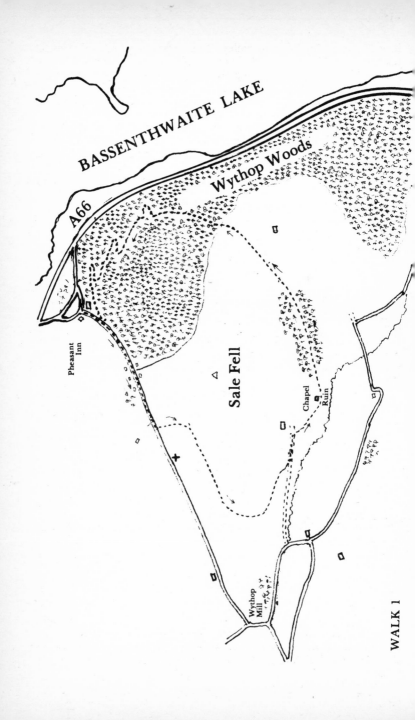

BASSENTHWAITE LAKE

A66

Wythop Woods

Pheasant Inn

Sale Fell

Chapel

Ruin

Wythop Mill

WALK 1

into the beautiful Wythop valley. The walk now is on a delightful terrace, and this green track descends to join a road, just over a wet area, before the farm buildings (Kelswick). This road goes up to the farm, but the walk goes up the track, opposite on the right.

This track rises a little and enters a wooded area. It then descends a little towards the remains of Wythop's old church. There is a view ahead of Skiddaw. The church was abandoned for a newer one, seen earlier in the walk, built in 1865 nearer the growing population. An inscription at the ruin suggests that the original church (then a chapel) was probably built about the 14th century, and was certainly there during the reign of Queen Mary (1553 - 1558). An open-air service is still held here in August.

Go on through the gate. There is an oak wood on the right with a bracken fell above on the left. When the track forks take the left-hand one which rises slightly. The way now goes through a delightful oak wood. There are glimpses of Skiddaw on the right, and these gradually open up to give better views. As the wood thins out there are pleasant views down into the green valley.

Presently a fainter track goes through a gate on the right and this should be ignored. Continue on a distinct path now, rising. The views improve as the walk continues on this pleasant green way. At the brow the view is magnificent. Below is a long stretch of Bassenthwaite Lake with Skiddaw behind. (There are a couple of wellplaced stone outcrops to sit on to take it all in at leisure.) On the right Keswick can be seen with a glimpse of the head of Derwent Water, with Walla Crag behind. Beyond is the Helvellyn range.

The way now goes into Wythop Woods through a gate (close it afterwards). A grass path is joined to begin with but this soon joins a forest road on a hairpin bend. Take the right-hand road down the hill. Now full marks to the Forestry Commission here. There is no vast acreage of sitka spruces but a delightful mixture of hardwoods and softwoods. As the way continues there is even a beech wood planted, right. The tree mixture means that there is also a variety of plants and flowers on the banks, with heather and bilberries and lichen. There are glimpses of Bassenthwaite Lake through the gaps. The forest road joins a T junction; turn right to continue descending. The road turns sharply left. When the next hairpin bend is reached continue onwards from the road onto a track left. There is a quarry soon on the left. The track now is green with some wet places. Now before this track rises look right for a path descending very sharply to the right. Shortly afterwards look for a better-defined green track zigging away sharp left. This track is joined by another coming from the left; continue on. In a short distance beyond this, zig right to join the track below. Turn right on it. You should see the Pheasant Inn through the trees on the left. Join the surfaced forest road and turn left along it. This rejoins the road near the Pheasant Inn where the walk started. Turn right to finish.

**4 miles [6.5 km]**

O.S. 1:50,000 Sheet No. 89

---

Loweswater is a gem. The view across its still water to the towering hump of Mellbreak epitomises all that is best in the Lake District landscape. It cannot be bettered if conditions are just right. Many motorists visit its northern shore briefly, unaware that, thanks to the National Trust, the far bank is a public access area where one can stroll or laze all day. There is a most pleasant walk all round the lake, only marred by the need to walk on a public (though slow) road for about half a mile.

The approach by road is normally by Lorton Vale, turning westwards as signposted, instead of going on to Crummock and Buttermere. An alternative approach from Cockermouth is off the A5086, turning eastwards after five miles, through Mockerkin. Just by the side of the road at the northern end of the lake is a grassy terrace where cars can be parked.

Leaving this grassy terrace, walk towards the foot of the lake (that is, south-east towards Mellbreak) along the road. After a short while it is possible to scramble down the bank through the trees to a path alongside the lake. Whether the shore can be comfortably walked or not depends on the height of the water. The wood here is a mixture of hardwoods (that is, broadleafed trees) and larches—conifers that lose their needles in winter. Along the shore, as usual, the pre-dominant tree is alder which likes to have its feet in wet places. Alder is fast-growing with wood that is light and easily worked. For this reason alders were commonly used in the old bobbin mills which used to thrive in the Lake District before the coming of plastic. Alder wood was much valued locally for other uses—clog soles, for instance.

There are some quite pretty scots pines further on, then the steepness of the bank, and wet ground, may force you back onto the road. Continue on the verge. Note some fine scots pines on the left of the road, mixed with other softwoods and some fine silver firs between the road and the lake further on. Just after a larch plantation on the left you can return by the National Trust sign to the lake shore again. Then a rude 'private' notice is reached at a fence. Go left up to the road through a gate.

Continue along the road in the same direction passing an old barn and a cottage. Among the stones in the roadside banks grow polypody fern. (Do not uproot!) These grow commonly in the thin

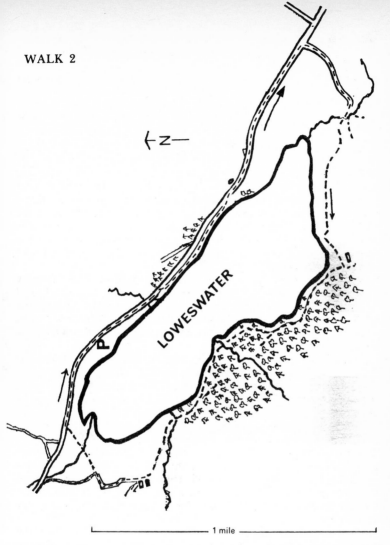

←—— 1 mile ——→

earth in walls and about tree-trunks. You pass the farm yard of Thrushbank on the left. Mellbreak is prominent right. Note how the hedges have been formed by the stems of the various trees being partly cut through and bent downwards to produce lateral growth. This art is known as 'laying' a hedge but locally it is known as 'liggin'. The hedge is a wild mixture of ash, hawthorn, hazel, holly and sycamore.

Presently a macadam lane joins from the right. Go right down this lane. After bends right, left, then right there is a gated lane on the right. A sign here indicates that this lane is a private road to Watergate and that cars cannot proceed. It is a bridleway however. Go through this gate and on towards Watergate, over a bridge, and on through the fields. Please note that you should keep to the bridleway here as this is valuable farmland and any gates you find closed, should be closed after you. Soon you have a pleasant view over the fields to the lake, then you reach Watergate. Go forwards, turn right through the gate, pass the sheepwash, and through another gate. A dirt lane goes pleasantly again by the shore and another gate brings you into National Trust property, Holme Wood. The wood is a splendid mixture of hardwoods, very colourful in autumn and spring. As usual, alders are in wet places but there are also chestnuts, elms, ash, sycamores, poplars, oaks, rowans and birches.

The lane begins to leave the lake slightly, but a narrow footpath leads off right, towards the lake, by a little building. Take this footpath. There are some aromatic grand firs, healthy juveniles, and shortly a chestnut which is far from juvenile. The leaves of the sweet chestnut are long and 'sawedged' and unlike the horse-chestnut are not arranged in circlets on the twigs. A beck has to be crossed. At the time of writing there is no footbridge but few people will have difficulty in striding across. Note the difference between the young birches and the mature. The older birches have silver trunks, often above a very gnarled bole; the youngsters have reddish stems rather like young cherry wood.

All about you is National Trust property and you can sit by this pleasant shore as long as you wish.

As you go on along the shore you reach the edge of the wood, at a wall and fence. Although a path can be seen going over the fence and across the field this is not a right of way. You should return to the bridleway, unless by the time you read this a new path has been made. The bridleway is through the trees on your left, and if in doubt find it by following the wall up. Having joined the bridleway turn right, go through a gate and right on. The bridleway continues up between walls and under oaks and you reach another farm, Hudson Place.

Turn right, under a 'weeping' larch, right through a gate and down a lane between banks and hedges. This lane curves left, then right near the foot of the hill, but just as it turns left there is a gate on the right. You now have a choice. You may take a short cut through this gate on a public footpath across dampish fields and a poor little footbridge minus handrail; or you can continue on down the bridleway to the road and turn right. The latter is straightforward. The former is described: go through the gate, forward over a slate culvert and on the same line towards the hedge. A stile and a little bridge can be seen. The footway is safe, the handrail is not. Nervous ladies may need help but it is only a short stride. Continue forward to the gate ahead alongside the road. Join the road and turn right to your starting point.

---

Crummock Water is Buttermere's larger sister. It has the same beauty that Buttermere is famed for; but wider, less intimate — and moody. Scenically it has almost everything; trees, moorland and rugged backgrounds and water that can be calm at one moment, and whipped white the next. It is magnificent. If photographers do this walk they will need a good supply of film and they will collect views that are not usually seen for they will visit some little known viewpoints. They are sublime.

There are, of course, snags. The quiet beaches on the west shore, offering the fine view of the water backed by the massive-looking hump of Grasmoor, need some effort to reach and wet feet are absolutely guaranteed. You could get back, as one fell-walking friend of mine puts it, with 'feet wet up to your waist'. Not to worry so long as your feet are warm and comfortable. So much for the big snag. What about the compensations? Well — great views; and quiet beaches far from the madding crowd.

You should consider this a full-day walk. Do not attempt a late afternoon start if you have an important dinner engagement. Best to have a morning start with a pack lunch. Much of the land en route, like the lake, is in the care of the National Trust or is open fell land with free access where you can stroll and loaf to your heart's content. An optional diversion is described which takes in Scale Force, a waterfall of over a hundred feet, but to avoid disappointment it should be said that the diversion is over rough ground and the fall is shut in a deep ravine and can only be nearly appreciated by a slimy scramble up wet rock and, at the time of writing, a rickety ladder. The descent out of the ravine is more dangerous than the ascent. Nevertheless even without the scramble to the near view the fall is quite impressive and in its way unique.

This walk should not be done when, after heavy and prolonged rain, the becks are in spate. As some of the land walked is rather remote, walkers who intend doing it alone should leave word with someone about the route. Otherwise it would be possible to sprain an ankle, for instance, and have to wait a very long time for someone to happen along and see you.

After reading this preamble it might be thought that the walk is something of epic proportions. It is certainly an adventure; but it is well within the capabilities of anyone who has limbered up on the

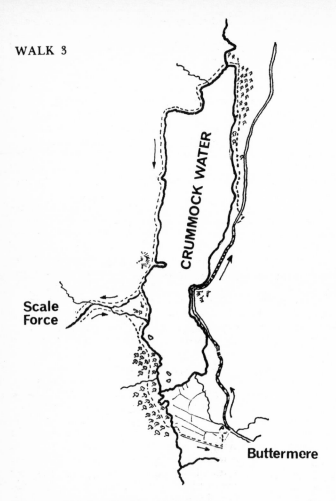

shorter walks described in this book.

The walk starts at Buttermere village. If the car parks are full there, drive westwards towards Cockermouth and there is a quarry car park on the right, and other odd places farther on.

Leave the village and walk along the roadside in the direction of Cockermouth. There are pleasant green fields then on the left, and an oak wood. Mixed plantings, mainly of the coniferous larch, and beech, and oak. You soon reach Wood House, set in a wood among oak and beech. You then descend towards the lake. There is a good view across with, at the far side, the fell of Mellbreak. Walk on the verge on the lake side of the road. Some way on there is a good view over your left shoulder with the craggy fells beyond Buttermere as the backcloth. Fleetwith Pike is on the left with Hay Stacks on the right. The nearer fell directly on the left has the odd name of Robinson. Further on you have a good view over the lake to Mellbreak. The little crag opposite is High Ling Crag.

Take care when the road reaches a point where it is fenced on the lake side. This is an excellent crag viewpoint at which to stop but you cannot proceed further except by the road. Keep close to the fence round the bend so that you can be seen by traffic coming both ways. After the fence finishes there is another little lake access point on the left. Believe it or not, this beach is the site of an old rubbish dump; local people are not usually so insensitive. The main part of the dump, across the road, has been soiled over, largely by volunteer labour.

You must now continue along the road, leaving the lake shore for a time. Walk on the grass verge on the right. Grasmoor towers above on the right. The crag immediately on your right which you are now leaving is Rannerdale Knott. All the land in view is composed of Skiddaw slate which usually breaks down into a kind of shale, producing softer outlines to the fells. But some of it, like the material of Rannerdale Knott, is quite hard. As you move forward there is another fell visible on the right. This is Whiteless Pike (2,159 feet). The ridge from it is Wandope, reaching the highest point at Crag Hill (2,749 feet). The verge finishes at a barn and house, right. Best keep to the right under three ash trees and on to a cottage. There is a pine plantation and a beck comes under the road. After this go over to the left, to keep on the outside of the next bend.

Your road walk soon finishes. There will be no more for the rest of the walk from the point where the wall on the right bends back, and there is a wide expanse of common grazing land, Cinderdale Common. Walk up onto it.

From the common there are good views of the lake. However, do not go far beyond the car parking areas made by the National Park Planning Board. Over the wall on the other side of the road you should see a wooden ladder-stile. Cross and climb over this and enter Fletcher Fields, the property of the National Trust. The lake shore can be reached by descending through the gorse bushes. Walk right, along the shore path, and note an old and shattered holly which appears to have a sapling growing right through it. Cross a little beck and walk along the shingle, or on grass at a higher level. The rocky terrain forces you back soon a short distance from the lake. Walk either side of a huge dead tree. There are alders, which usually grow in wet ground, by the lake shore. Cross the beck.

Shortly the path narrows and continues just above the lake. It then goes close to the lake shore again among oak, birch and alder. A poor stile is reached at a wall but there is a better one up the wall side to the right. You are now in another oak grove. There is a stile in a wall again or you can walk round the wall end. The margin of the lake is now wet and you proceed above this. You pass some hazel shrubs and continue on a green footpath with Grasmoor towering, forward on the right. Go on under a large oak tree, across a little beck and enter a plantation, through a little stile. The planting is largely of douglas fir and larch.

Going on through the wood you come to another stile with stepping stones across a beck just before it and into another wood planted with scots pine and other trees among them. Below is a boat house and boat landing. You join a substantial track flanked with heather.

The ground falls steeply between the track and the lake. This area has a natural growth of hardwoods. Up on the right European larch have been planted above the hardwoods. Farther on pines grow between the track and the lake end. There is a path junction on the left; take this. You can see a very fine view up the lake. Stroll right round the foot of the lake over the two footbridges erected by the local water board. There are grand views all the way. Rannerdale Knott is the prominent point opposite, on the left of it is Grasmoor. Cross a beck by another footbridge and continue on round a concrete parapet and observe another example of waterworks architecture — this time a round-house.

Continue on the concrete parapet, stepping over wire at the end. Here there are a number of pines — this time not scots but austrian pines, or black pines. The cones are larger than the scots and the trunks not as reddish. Continue on with the fence parallel to the lake shore. This comes onto a shingle beach which is also a good viewpoint. Go over two stiles, over a fence and a wall (both poor). There is still a delightful beach. You go through another stile which is very poor, then you must move inland to avoid wet ground. A green path can be picked up. This is fairly wet before it goes back to the lake shore. You are now really in some wild moorland. Cross the remnants of a stile in a broken wall. As you go on you will observe some of the wildness is tamed. This is because Mellbreak, the great fell on the right, offers some shelter from strong winds. Even the grass grows differently.

The beach continues very fine. You cross what appears to be waste from an old mine working. Anciently there must have been several points on this shore where ore was extracted and was probably taken by boat to the far shore for smelting on Cinderdale Common. Go on, through some gorse bushes eventually. A wet section after this can probably be best avoided by taking to the gravel of the lake shore. A plain path can then be seen at a higher level. Beware of the slippery wet rock.

A rocky spur is reached. The path over it is a bit of a scramble and it is easier to by-pass it by the lake shore below. The path crosses a broken fence and heads right a little but does not, as might appear from here, go to the right of the big crag in front. It crosses above a bog, then it goes forward below this crag, High Ling Crag. Now children will want to rush forward onto the narrow peninsula. Why not? This is indeed a very pleasant shingly viewpoint. Low Ling Crag. The depth on either side of the peninsula is over 120 feet and you can see how steeply the rock dips down on the up-lake side.

Going back to your path you reach a flattish area between fells. Go on through some wetness to a large beck with a broken wall on its far side and at this point you must decide whether you are to divert to look at Scale Force. You are now about a mile and a half from home. The diversion is over half a mile and the ground is rough. The diversion is described first. If you wish to continue shore-ward pick up the directions after the next paragraph.

To reach Scale Force you have to go up right with the beck without crossing it yet. This means progress over a very wet portion just before the beck. Whatever you do *do not try to avoid this by going up right.* You could go in very deep on seemingly easy ground. It is marginally better to go down a little to the left. Having reached the beck side go right, with it, and right, round a sheepfold. Continue on past what looks like an old ruined sheepfold, possibly a building, on the left. Another view back at Crummock here, offering yet another mood. A fence corner is reached. Do not go through the gate but go on to the left of the fence. Further up the path gets narrow, eroded and wet. A landslide further on forces you to the beck side. The nasty barbed wire fence gradually forces you to the beck and eventually you must cross it at a suitable narrow point. Continue following the beck, this time on the other side. Scale Force now creeps into sound and view. A better green path is picked up which leads you on up, and then down to cross a plank bridge. The falls can then be approached on the left and you have a view of them up the narrow gully. Above on the left of the falls' foot is another old mine waste heap. This ore is in the middle of the beck which marks the boundary of the Skiddaw slate and the harder granophyre, a later volcanic rock. Having seen the falls descend on this side of the beck, with a fine view ahead. The path gets plainer lower down and you pass an old sheep pen. Up above on the right is Red Pike. There is a wet section and the path turns right, and then comes another wet section crossed by stepping stones. The next paragraph describes the walk along the lake shore from the point where you diverted.

To continue along the lake shore from the point where you reached the beck, go left over very wet ground until you can cross the beck. Here you will notice that the beach gravel is quite different. It is granophyre of which Red Pike, up above on the right, and the fells beyond are composed. It was formed from volcanic action after the Skiddaw slate was laid down. The shingle has, in fact, changed dramatically in a few feet. Observe traces of an old jetty which was probably connected with the old iron mine working far up the fell above.

You come to a beck. If you cannot cross it here go further up to a point where it divides into two and you should be able to cross the two narrower channels. Go back and continue by the lake shore. There are some hardwoods growing and there is another beck to cross, followed by another with slippery stepping stones and then several more small becks. You come to a little rock face. Struggle up the right here and go up between the holly and the rowan. Continue on the top of the crag, to the right of a boulder, cross a boggy section up on the right — well up, where a sheep trod can be seen crossing it. Go towards the trees ahead. Observe little Scale Island off shore here. There are rowans and hollies and you go forward to strike a green footpath, the one from Scale Force.

Go on through the mixed hardwoods, cross a little beck. All the rowans (mountain ash) around here are somewhat old for rowans. Observe two more islands ahead in the lake. There is a wet section and the path goes left. You cross a beck and another boggy section and then go right to cross yet another boggy section. You come in left again to pick up a slightly better path and cross another beck to the right of an old sheepfold. This crossing is a bit nasty. Beyond you join a better path. The path is stony and there is another beck to cross. Below now the lake has ended and the river joining it to Buttermere makes a snakelike coil. After another beck look for the oaken sculpture on the left. Birch and ash have colonised the rough rocks above on the right. The path rises slightly and curves right under oaks, and there are some large rocks which have broken away from the fell; probably after the fell-sides were undermined by the cutting glacier.

You now come across Scale Bridge, a pretty arch-bridge with two arches, one small. This is a fine piece of rural architecture, best seen from the other side. Cross the bridge and continue on the track beyond. The track swings left and heads for Buttermere village. The fields are always lush and green here. Go through two gates to a T junction with a hard track. Turn left and this brings you, no doubt with wet feet but glowing with health and happy satisfaction, past the Fish Hotel and back to your car.

---

Rannerdale is a hidden dale concealed by the Rannerdale Knotts and Low Bank; a hump of land of hard Skiddaw slate thrusting into the head of Crummock Water. It is rarely visited yet is a delightful and quite typical lakeland dale. Those enthusiasts who have read Nicholas Size's *The Secret Valley* will be eager to visit the scene of the great battle between the Norman army under Ranulf and the Norse settlers under Earl Boethar.

This walk should be done in clear weather for the views are excellent. Smooth-soled footwear could be dangerous as the walk ends in a fairly steep descent on grass. There are one or two wet patches which can be avoided with care. There is free access to the open fell land of Rannerdale and you can take a picnic and/or a good book and spend a quiet few hours there.

The start is at Buttermere village. If the car parks are full try driving towards Crummock and Cockermouth. There is a little quarry car park just outside the village and one or two other small places. Walk on towards Crummock. (That is, north-west.) About half a mile from the village centre, the road takes a turn and Crummock Water comes into view, and there is a lane off between iron fences on the right which is in fact the line of the old road. Take this. There is a mixed wood with larch and spruce between you and the road left. The path rises, and then descends to rejoin the road. You turn a corner and Crummock Water is before you.

Before the road descends to the side of the lake, there is a green track going off along the fell side to the right. Take this. It is on the line of the old road which existed before the present one was blasted out around the corner of Rannerdale Knott. The way begins to gain height giving pleasant views over the lake at once. The fell at the other side on the left is Red Pike (2,479 feet) which sits behind a smaller peak. When the path levels out, look back. The largest fell, on the left up valley, has the strange name of Robinson. Behind that you can see the Pike of Fleetwith, above Honister. To the right of that are knobbly summits called Hay Stacks, then right of that again is the ridge of High Pike and High Stile. Walk on and the path rises more gradually. Ahead are the steep crags of Mellbreak at the other side of Crummock Water. Ignore the turnings from the path which go up the fell and when the path forks go left. Soon you are on Rannerdale Knott.

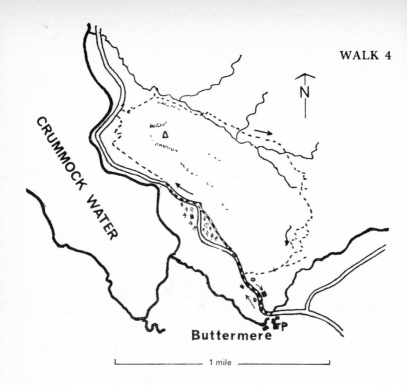

Cross the shoulder of rock and descend a little. If you look at this rock you should see that we are on what was once a cart road, for the wheel wear is still apparent. This would have been the only way up the valley before the rock below was blasted out for the new road. Just after this you descend. Ignore the sheep trods going off right. Detour left up the rock knoll from which point you can see almost all of Crummock Water. Go back to the track, and continue the descent. You should be able to make out the zig-zags of the old road. The old way, however, is wet now and it is advisable to keep to the left of it. Go sharp left first past the first zig-zag then over a little knoll and continue down the path. Beware on the steep steps. Pick your own way down. The way betters as you get lower. Rejoin the road.

You leave the road, right, almost at once, walking between Rannerdale Knott on your right and a wall, left. The rock has been quarried on the right, mainly for dry-stone walls. There is the site of an old rubbish dump, too. Go through the gate and continue with the wall until the wall corner is reached, and the path goes forward, before curving right to go up the valley. The peak which you see ahead as you go up the valley is Whiteless Pike. Rannerdale Knott, from this side, also looks spectacular. A beck will be seen on the left and the path follows it. This is

24

Rannerdale Beck. Most of the place names in this area are Norse; 'Ranner' was probably a Norse worthy, and this was his dale.

The path comes closer to the beck, the water of which is crystal-clear. For a time the path is rocky. Ash grow on the other beck bank and above on the right mountain ash are clinging characteristically to the rock face. Holly is growing on the face, too. The berry seeds will have been dropped into crevices by birds. Continue by the beck past dead rowans. The path goes on between the beck, left, and a wall, right. Rannerdale Beck comes down from the fell opposite, and the beck you are now following is Squat Beck. A little way up this beck, cross it by the stepping-stones and follow it up on the opposite bank. Continue up on the higher land on the left, still following this smaller beck. There is no clear path at this point.

Cross the line of an old broken wall. You now stand on the battlefield of *The Secret Valley* and you can imagine the Norse reinforcements coming down the gullies where they had been hiding — there would have doubtless also been more tree cover then, rowans and oaks. The valley holds a surprisingly grassy plain, an ideal pasture as well as a battlefield. Keep the beck in view on the right. Cross an old slate bridge, over a little beck, go through a gateway with old stone gateposts, then to avoid the worst of some wetness go left of the rushy area, then move over towards the fence, and follow it. You come to a poor stile. Cross the beck, and incline left up the green path. Continue on the same course as you have come so far, going towards the pass in the fells above. Ignore the sheep trods going up the fell; the slope of the current path is gentle.

The path presently meanders and goes left of a boggy area and you find yourself walking on what looks like a man-made causeway. It is probably the remains of an ancient wall. You cross the beck again with the path over a muddy area; best to go left of the worst patch. Proceed up the beck on the other bank. The path zig-zags and crosses another very old wall. This was a ditch-and-wall arrangement. It may have been a defensive wall; but in fact ancient cattle enclosures are sometimes found with a wall-and-ditch fence. Continue on with the beck which is now only a ribbon of water.

The path is rather a fag now as it rises. Take your time, if necessary with plenty of rests. There is a sheep pen on the right. Now beware of a wet section on the path. Go up to the left above it. The nastiest wetness is directly opposite the sheep fold, and can be distinguished by the brighter green of the grass and moss. You can go in here above your knees! The path narrows but is fairly clear on the ground. The way becomes smoother and drier as you go higher. The beck now vanishes and there is only a bog.

Now look back. You can see over Crummock and over to Loweswater. If there is great clarity you can see even beyond — to the Solway.

Go through the pass and facing you is the huge side of Robinson. Over on the right is a view over Buttermere with the long ribbon of Sourmilk Gill pouring down the hillside.

Now go right, descending to a knoll summit. From here you have a bird's eye view of the foot of Buttermere and the head of Crummock. From this point to Buttermere the fell side is 'stepped' with a series of crags like the knoll you are standing on. It is not a good idea, then, to make a direct descent. You should go either to the left or the right of these steps for paths go down either side. Do not descend direct to the paths but walk back along the fell side, descending to them slowly. When either of the paths is reached you will find that for a time they are still fairly steep. *Take your time*. Do not allow children to run as they can soon lose control and fall heavily.

The paths both on the right and on the left join at the bottom of the rocky steps. The path then goes left to join another path alongside a wall. Follow this down behind the cottages and join the road. Buttermere village is on the left.

---

In the romantic period of tourism in the Lake District the pundits declared that Buttermere offered the summit of pure perfection of landscape. Everyone who thought himself a connoisseur of scenery raved about this rural paradise, this lone green valley set among the 'awful' mountains. Nothing has changed; only human attitudes. We are rather less inclined to sentimentality about rural life and a little more objective in our views about scenery. If we no longer regard mountains as 'awful' the most blasé among us would admit that the head of Buttermere and its western skyline is dramatic. Buttermere is set in the smooth-lined alpine landscape of the Skiddaw shale but at its head and to the west rear the hard-lined crags of the Borrowdale volcanic series, and the rugged granophyre. At the head, above Honister Pass, the hard volcanic ash which created the slate beds has a distinctive green colour which has made the quarries famous. The lake, too, at certain times of the year has a distinctly green appearance; at other times a deep blue. The scene is set about by fine trees, and bracken, moss and lush green grass, heather and tumbling white water. 'Look back, lass', says a local down-to-earth character, known to the author, to his wife as he motors off on his annual holiday, 'for whatever we see on holiday won't cap that for beauty.'

This, then, is a 'must' for everyone. The walk round the lake offers one of the Lake District's finest treats. The western shore — the farthest from the road — is in the care of the National Trust which also owns the lake itself. You can therefore wander freely on the western side and sit by the lake there as long as you like. All lake shore paths are bound to have wet sections and this is no exception (although one day a volunteer work party could do a lot of good on the western section.) Otherwise the walk should offer no problems to young or old.

Park in Buttermere village. Starting the walk from the square in the village between the Bridge Hotel and the Fish Hotel, a track leads lake-wards on the left-hand side of the Fish. Go down the track which soon turns left, between fences. Go through the kissing-gate. Ignore the signposted path to Scale Force. After the kissing-gate go right between fences. Ahead is the long string of a waterfall on the fell side; this is Sourmilk Gill. After heavy rain its name seems appropriate. The stream flows out of a little tarn between the peaks

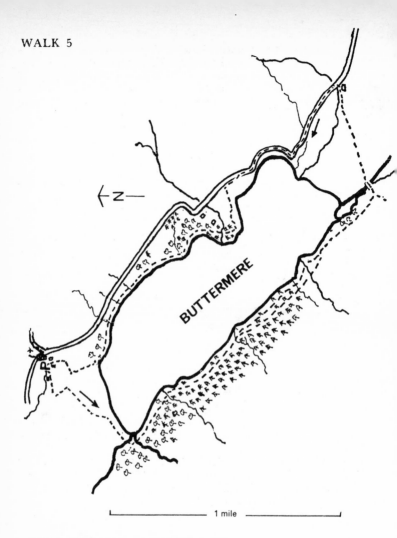

BUTTERMERE

←z—

1 mile

of High Stile, left, and Red Pike, right.

You come to a gate and stile. Go through either and then turn right, following the fence. From this point now you can see right up the lake to Fleetwith Pike, the more dominant peak, above Honister. Cross the footbridge and go forward on the path beyond. Go over some rough cobbles, bearing left. Cross the beck by the plank bridge and go over the tall ladder-stile. You now turn left; but if you wish to have a closer look at the foot of Sourmilk Gill go up the bank and over the next ladder-stile first, and then return. (The fall foot is probably only worth looking at after wet weather.)

28

Go on the lake shore path. After a short time this rises to a slightly higher level, into woodlands. Larch are planted here among the hardwoods. The path joins a wider track. As you walk see if you can spot the sweet chestnut (or spanish chestnut) trees, with the long saw-edged leaves. These look fine in autumn. Cross a little footbridge and go through a gateway across a little beck into a larch plantation. The path goes to the lake shore again.

Cross another small footbridge, and then come to wet sections before you pass alongside a spruce plantation. The path reaches a little bay, where there is a stream to cross. The house across the lake is Hassness, in the ownership of the Lake District National Park and let to the Ramblers' Association as a guest house. You have a choice at this point. You can continue along the lake shore on a rather rough, wet path; or you can go up to a better path on a higher level. The two paths link farther along, after the lake shore one has obliged the walker to negotiate an awkward stile. The higher-level path only needs description.

From this little bay go upwards to the right. Go up through the spruce plantation up some rocky steps. Follow the path on through the tree gap. There is a short wet section and the path rises soon to a plain track. Turn left along it. The track rises a little and then flattens out. There is a mixed planting hereabouts of norway spruce (christmas trees) and sitka spruce. The latter have a greyer appearance and their needles are prickly. Soon there is a larch plantation with some pines, and then after this there are sitka spruce with some oaks, on the right. You leave the wood by a wicket gate. The crag soaring up on the right is High Crag. As you go forward there are trees over a wall left. Cross a slate bridge and the path continues at a higher level with the bracken below. You look forward into the dramatic valley head with the heights of Hay Stacks on the right and Fleetwith Pike on the left.

The path now turns left through a gate and you go on over a footbridge with a beautiful view down the lake. There is a wet section before the next gate. (Be sure to close these gates.) Follow the fence. Go through a gateway and on with the fence. Follow the fence on the right, towards the farm-yard of Gatesgarth. Go through the gates, on through the farmyard and then onto the road.

Go left. Soon a view of the fells over the lake opens up. A comb opposite (a hollow between two craggy peaks) scooped out by a glacier in the ice age is Burtness Comb, a popular climbing ground. The peak on its left is High Crag, and the one on the other side of the comb is High Side (2,644 feet.) Beyond that is another comb out of which flows Sourmilk Gill and on the right of it is Red Pike, a pointed peak of 2,479 feet. The road goes alongside the lake. Close to the shore the ground is boggy, however, so you will need to continue on the grass verge by the road. Soon, though, you will see two stone gate posts on the left and a track leading from this point towards the lake shore. Go left down here. Go over the poor stile by the gate and continue left close to the lake. There is no clear path on the grass here—you just go along the shore. Go round the end of the wall under the ash tree and reach a fine promontory covered in pine and beech. This is another excellent and much-photographed view; Shingle Point on the Hassness estate owned by the National Park.

From here go on across a little footbridge by a beech tree badly scarred by initials. You now go along a terrace path and over a stile. This path was made by the one-time owner of Hassness for his private enjoyment. You will soon see his pride and joy—a tunnel cut through the rock. A local tale has it that the owner did not like to see his outdoor staff idle in wet weather, and this is one job he had them do.

At the far end of the tunnel go over a stile and continue on the lake shore. Go through an iron wicket gate after which the path rises a little from the lake shore. There is a good specimen of another sweet chestnut soon.

Cross a stile and continue on by the path just above the shore. Go across another stile at the end. Now follow the fence on the right, go over a little slate bridge and go right, with a beck. After a short distance cut the corner left towards a large stone slab and go up the rock steps and through a wooden wicket gate and then go up right with the fence. A track is joined on which turn left. Go through a gate and on through the farmyard. You are then back in the village.

O.S. 1:50,000 Sheet No. 89

---

This is a walk for those with an urgent need to burn up some calories fast or who are doing penance for some previous self-indulgence. On a map it does not look far. But a map is flat. An American acquaintance climbing with the author up a craggy cliff once said, 'The scenery around here is slightly perpendicular.' This is a fair description of this walk. It is not for people with heart conditions or for those who go dizzy at the top of step-ladders. Otherwise, with perseverance, and older folk taking more time, it is not impossible. The walk starts from a waterfall, climbs up very steeply through a forest, onto a forest road, and then goes pleasantly through the silent trees to descend a wooded fell.

The walk starts from Whinlatter Pass on the B5292 Cockermouth to Keswick road via Lorton. The road climbs out of the village of Lorton and just before turning sharply right over a bridge after one mile there is a lay-by on the left. By it is a footpath sign, of motorway proportions, pointing to 'Spout Force'. After seeing this sign one would assume that the waterfall was at least the size of Niagara. It is in fact quite modest—but pretty. The beck which forms the fall is Aiken Beck (which probably sounds as how you might feel if you tackled this walk in too much haste!)

Park in the lay-by and walk through the kissing-gate. Follow the path alongside the wall and go through the next kissing-gate. The path, guided by another 'motorway sign', goes down to the beck and follows it up. Japanese larch are planted above us on the left. At the opposite side of the beck are Norway spruce (christmas trees). As you go higher sitka spruce mix in with the larch and become thicker. The path goes close to the beck, then inclines left up through the sitkas—almost a tree tunnel. The path goes on steeply. Avoid wetness by going left although a turning right is a detour for nimble people with good footwear who want a close look at the foot of the waterfall. Those doing so should return to the tree tunnel again.

The path goes up through Norways and comes to an old sign which announces that you have reached the end of the public footpath. Just after this you have the view of the falls. It is not a full view and the perch is rather precarious. The new policy of the Forestry Commission allows you to proceed beyond the end of the public footpath so continue on up the path above. The first few

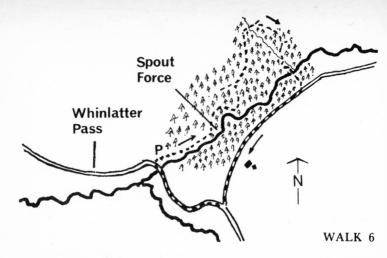

**Spout Force**

**Whinlatter Pass**

P

N

steps are rather high and awkward. You come to a slab of rock; go left and over this and continue climbing. You now have a bird's-eye view of the sitkas. Look for their hanging cones. Go forward through the tree tunnel. Cross an open area and continue through another tunnel. After crossing a drainage channel the way goes left along an avenue straight up through the trees. This reaches the beck side and from now you go steeply up hill. This goes even steeper. Carry on with frequent rests. Trees about here are norways now — softer than the prickly and greyer sitkas. Eventually daylight is seen at the end of the tunnel and the despairing will take heart. At the end you scramble up an almost vertical bank and collapse onto a forest road.

After getting back your breath go right and enjoy a less arduous walk. Sitkas are now on the right and larch on the left. Farther on there are larch on both sides. The fell ahead is Broom Fell. The road bears right and there are spruces at the corner. On reaching a junction, turn right and enjoy a gradual descent through the silent wood (unless there are chain saws working hereabouts!). The road goes round a hairpin bend. Continue on down it. A branch road comes in from the left but continue straight on. There is soon an open area left and a group of farm buildings. Most of the farmland has been swallowed up by planting and Darling How is no longer a farmhouse. Go down over the cattle grid and find yourself in more open country as you approach the road.

Turn right at the road and continue on the verge. Go on the outside of the bend so that you can be seen by traffic from both directions. Cross over to the outside of the next bend. Note how the trees in the ravine on the left have grown tall in a rapid search for light. Cross again to the outside of the next bend, and you are back at the starting point.

**7¼ miles [11.5 km]**

O.S. 1:50,000 Sheet No. 89

---

Ennerdale is the least visited of the major lakes, yet it is superb. The view up-lake to the rugged valley head, on a clear day, cannot be bettered anywhere. The approaches to it deter most tourists. It is out on a limb away from the circular routes and the major roads. The approach roads are narrow and devious and traverse dull rolling country quite untypical of the Lake District. The fells and mountains that *are* typical start in the west at the foot of Ennerdale Water — but what a start!

There is access to the greater part of the lake shore. Most tourists are content to park their cars at the two car parks at the lake foot and seldom wander far from them. The walk described goes right round the lake. Compared with the other walks in this book this one is something of a marathon. It is not so much the distance as the rough terrain. The granophyre, the local rock here, breaks into blocks, and much of the walk — a bit less than half of it — is over rock-litter thinly covered in turf, some of it wet. This cannot be walked over in a hurry and if you are to enjoy the walk regard this as a day's expedition with a pack lunch. Footwear should be able to stand up to the rugged ground and anyone with a poor head for heights will not enjoy one short section. It is not a good idea to do the walk alone but if you insist on walking alone it is wise to leave word of your route with someone so that you can be easily found in the event of a mishap.

The walk starts at the car park made by the Forestry Commission near Bowness Point. To reach this you need to get to Croasdale. Approaching from the west via Cleator Moor follow the signs for Ennerdale Bridge. From here you drive eastwards still (the sign at Ennerdale Bridge directs you to 'Crossdale'). Ignore the sign for Ennerdale Lake and you will reach the crossroads which are practically all there is at Croasdale. (The ring above the signpost here also spells it 'Crossdale'). Take the sign for 'Roughton', going south-east towards the lake. The road is narrow and as you follow it on you cross a cattle-grid onto a Forestry Commission road. The car park is on the left before you get to the Commission's gate by a sign saying that the road is private.

Croasdale is reached from the Cockermouth direction from the Cockermouth to Cleator Moor road (A5086); take the sign for 'Lamplugh' and then 'Croasdale' (spelt correctly from this direction). Then follow the directions as in previous paragraph.

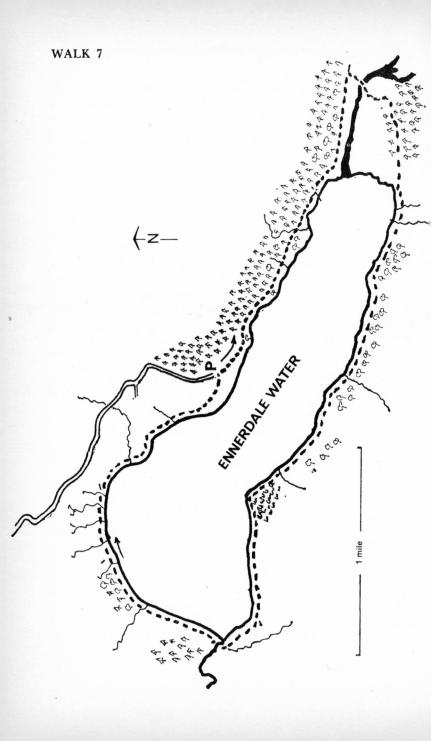

ENNERDALE WATER

1 mile

Between the car park and the lake is a knoll, Bowness Point. This is a public access area and is a good place from which to start the walk. From the summit, across the lake can be seen Anglers' Crag. Walk left and forward to the lake shore side and walk along the shore on one of the paths. That is, left, up the lake. After a while the way leads you onto the Forestry road. Continue on. The first planting you see is of larch. Further on on the left there are spruces. As you near the head of the lake a beck crosses under the road and through a promontory. The beck is Smithy Beck and as the name might suggest there was once an ancient rural industry here.

You reach the head of the lake, but carry on along the forest road. The river which feeds Ennerdale Water is the Liza, and it snakes along on its relatively flat gravel beds on the right. Pillar Fell dominates the forward view (2,927 feet). To its right is the peak of Steeple (2,687 feet) and then right again the rounded summit of Haycock (2,618 feet). Beeches have been planted on the left — poor specimens of little timber value. Shortly a footbridge will be seen across the river below, just after the road rises. A steep track will be seen leading down to a gate near the bridge. Take this track, go over the stile alongside the gate and over the footbridge. Bear left and go through the large gap in the wall and follow the fence on your left.

The going is fairly easy here. You are walking on a bed of silt deposited by the Liza over the centuries. Looking over to your right to the fells on the northern side of the lake is Great Borne and Starling Dodd, a hump of fell just over 2,000 feet, which separates Ennerdale from Crummock. At the fence end follow the wall on. You come to a corner of a Forestry plantation. Now from this point most walkers follow the wall on all the way to the lake head but this is not a right of way and involves climbing a fence. It cannot therefore be recommended and the following route more closely follows the right of way. Go through the gate into the plantation where the trees are scots pines. Go right up through the gap in the pines until you come to a more open area where the planting changes to larch. A branch path now leaves on the right. This is the route. The path which you leave rises steeply beyond this junction, so if you find yourself climbing you have gone too far!

Having turned right go on through the gap between the larches. After about fifty yards there is a more open area. The path appears to go right on across wet ground but there is a fainter path branching off on drier ground to the right; take this. It is rather obscured by bracken at first, simply because people are not using this right of way. You find yourself walking between the light green larches on the right and a darker planting of sitka spruce on the left. The path descends and then there are pines on the right and the spruce still left. Soon there are larches again on the right. The lake can be glimpsed ahead over the tree tops. At the end of this path a 'lift open' gate (partially obstructed by wire) is reached. Go through this and close the gate after you.

You must now walk on more difficult ground, with lumpy rocks and wet turf. Go through the wall gap and along the path which you can see faintly in the bracken. This path keeps to the left of a wet area and close to rising ground. Keep on the path and do not be tempted to the lake shore too soon. The going is rough, all 'heads down and knees up'. Eventually you come to a mountain ash tree; keep to the bracken below this and make for the lake shore path, going over the muddy sections as best you can on stepping stones. The going becomes a little drier further on and the path is more easily seen. Cross a beck, go through a wall gap, and keep to the left to avoid the worst of a wet patch straight ahead. Cross two more becks and you are into a birch wood. As you continue there are several little becks to cross. Eventually you reach a wall. Go through the wicket gate and continue on and ford a beck. The way continues very rough. At last you leave the wood, and are among heather patches.

You are now more than half way on your walk. The ground steepens to the lake here and the path rises a little. Keep to the upper path and you soon see a well in front. There is a gap through it and if you are too low you will have to move up to the left towards it. Go on along the path beyond the gap. You are now more or less opposite Bowness Point, behind which your car is parked and if you left granny sitting by the lake shore there you can wave to her. Now a crag can be seen on the path ahead and the path looks impossible alongside it. It looks a little better at closer quarters. Before tackling it look back at the beautiful head of the lake. On the other side of the valley on the extreme right are the back of Red Pike and High Stile which wall in Buttermere.

The path climbs towards the crag (Anglers' Crag) and goes over scree (loose stones). It looks more difficult than it is, though timid females may need reassurance. The path falls to go below a spur of rock, then climbs again for a short section. It again descends and climbs to go over a rough step. This is not difficult. If it makes you nervous remember that it is all in the mind; if this was in your garden rockery at home you would not be in the least afraid! The path bends left between a boulder and the fellside, and you go down a rock step. (Some people may prefer to do this on their backsides.) The path then descends to the lake shore, and the worst is over.

Watch your feet, though, because the way continues rough. It eases after a while and there are only boulder patches. The beach here is very attractive if you need a rest. On reaching a wall cross it by a wooden ladder stile and a beck by a stone slab. You approach another architectural gem of the sort for which water boards are famous. These edifices are supposed to blend in with the natural surroundings. This one is made of local stone and slate — for which all praise — but the architect was no doubt much-travelled for his building seems to have been inspired by a public convenience in a Japanese tea garden.

Go through a gate on the path, then through a second gate and over the bridge. The waterworks weir is to the right. Go through the gate at the other side of the bridge and over a wet section. Make your way to a stone causeway which has been built over a muddy section on your right. This does not quite make the dry ground on the far side at the moment, but it is a help. A reasonable path is picked up on the lake shore. There is another fine view up lake. If you look at the lake gravel here you will see that it is now largely composed of grey shale — Skiddaw slate. Boggy sections can be avoided by a wettish path to the left. You reach a gate. Go through it and continue by the lake shore on a green track. A hard lane joins the track from the left and you approach spare ground now used as a car park.

Continue on now on easier walking. Attempts were made to retain the lake shore trees by building concrete banks round them but this has not been completely successful. Some of them are dying. Go through the gate. Continue on the lake shore pebbles if you have a mind to do so, but you will have to move back to the track at a wall farther on, for there is a gate here. Go through this gate and turn immediately right down the stony track back to the lake. Continue on a most pleasant dry green path. Cross a footbridge, then avoid the wetness by walking on the concrete wall. There is another footbridge which, like the first, was erected by volunteer labour.

A bridge of concrete sleepers is crossed near a huge dead ash trunk by the lake shore. The track then reaches a broken wall which is the boundary of Bowness Point from which you started. A path starts off between stone walls on the left but avoid the first wet section of it by going above it on the bank on the right. Enjoy a last view of the lake which looks great from here if there is a colourful sunset. Rejoin the path further along and continue on to the car park.

O.S. 1:50,000 Sheet No. 89

---

The land erosion which came on the heels of the ice age smoothed the landscape down evenly to the West Cumberland coast. But one up-tilted jutting shelf of sandstone was by-passed south of Whitehaven. This is now known as St Bees Head. It ends at the sea with cliffs of over 300 feet. A path round its rim offers an exhilarating walk. There is much to interest bird watchers. St Bees Head is a nature reserve cared for by the Royal Society for the Protection of Birds. Among the birds which nest on the cliff are guillemots, fulmars, razorbills and kittiwakes. Of course this walk is not for those who are afraid of heights and it should not be attempted in strong winds. Footwear should have good well-cleated soles; even so, sections of the path are slippery after rain, but the path is not really dangerous. A slip would end in loss of dignity, not life!

The walk is a longish one, and it is one of those which could well be done when carrying a picnic meal. After about a quarter of the route has been completed you can descend into a cove and have your meal on the beach. But walkers should be warned not to wander far from the mouth of the cove if the tide is coming in as they could very easily be trapped. Children also may need to be warned not to try cliff climbing. Having given these dire warnings it should be said that this walk is an adventure and well worth the effort and you might add to it by inspecting the lighthouse. This, of course, requires permission from the keeper, who might make a small charge. Admission is at his discretion and if he has an emergency to deal with naturally he will not be anxious to make your acquaintance.

The walk starts at the village of St Bees, quaint but unlovely. It is outside the National Park for some reason; otherwise the caravan site near the beach might have been re-sited and better screened. Park at the car park near the beach at St Bees. The village is reached from several points on the Whitehaven to Millom road (A595) as signposted. It is west of the town of Egremont.

Walk to the shore and along it to the right. Bear right, then cross the footbridge. Turn left and go over the stile, right. Follow the path along the edge, continuing over another stile and on. The path then divides and you can go either way. The path on the right with the fence offers easier walking; the one on the left

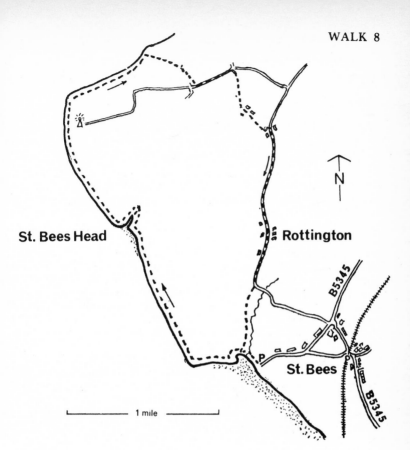

St. Bees Head

Rottington

B5345

St. Bees

B5345

N

1 mile

probably gives better views. When the lighthouse eventually comes into sight, go right of the fence and on through stiles with a good view of the cliffs ahead. The way now is barred by a cove.

This is Fleswick Bay. The descent into it is steep, and also slippery if the path is wet. Alas, the cove is a regular rubbish receptacle in its narrows, most of the trash being pushed in and left by the sea. Perhaps someone will do a great service by firing the driftwood and burning all the plastic and rubber on it? As you walk out, where the seas wash, all is clean. Looking at the cliffs of red sandstone one is baffled perhaps by the unusual effect of red walls and grey-pebbled floor. Some of the huge sandstone slabs at the cliff-foot have been smoothed by pounding pebbles into unusual and artistic shapes. The whole area is an artist's dream — but this is surrealism; a weird blend of the starkly material and the extravagantly abstract. Semi-precious stones can sometimes be picked up on this beach. To the author all wet, coloured pebbles are something very special so no advice on recognition can be given here.

To leave this bay go back into the narrows. On the left you will see footholds cut into the rock and there should be a wire to pull yourself up with. This short ascent is not too difficult but if you are deterred the other way out is to retrace your steps up the path by which you descended. At the bank top turn left and head for the gate. Go through the gate and bear left to avoid wet ground, then left again along the fringe of the bay to pick up a path which continues at a level higher than the path from the bottom by the cut steps.

Now follow the path by the fence along the cliff edge to the lighthouse. Continue on along the cliff edge. From this point in clear weather you could well see the Isle of Man and the Irish coast. Right forward you should see across the Solway to the hills of Kirkcudbright in Scotland. The path descends into a small gully. (This could be wet in the bottom.) There is an easy ascent out of it through a small ravine. Continue on until the path is barred by a fence. First look may make you apprehensive as it would appear that you will be forced into the sea. However, look closer and there is a stile. Go over this and continue alongside the fence. (Ignore the stile in it on the left.) A wall is reached. Turn right with it, for at this point you leave the cliffs and head inland. You reach a gate. Go through this and onto a lane between walls. A road is met at crossroads. Turn left.

Continue on for about a quarter of a mile and take the first turning on the right, a stony lane. Observe the winding gear of a pit head on the left, for you are on the edge of a coalfield. The red sandstone overlays the coal which was once the main industry of Whitehaven, which is now only a couple of miles away. There are views up through the Ennerdale fells on the left. Go round left by the cottages. There is a finely-built barn at the end. You descend on a lane overhung with trees. The road is joined at a sharp angle. Turn sharp right. Now go along the road. There is over a mile of road walking but it is not at all unpleasant as the road is not a busy one. It is tree-fringed and there is running water first right then left. You enter the old village of Rottington.

Continue on past a row of bungalows. Then the road takes a sharp turn to the left but in the bend angle on the right is a gate. Go through this and follow the wall and hedges over stiles all the way to the footbridge at the start.

**3½ miles [5.5 km]**

O.S. 1:50,000 Sheets Nos. 89 and 96

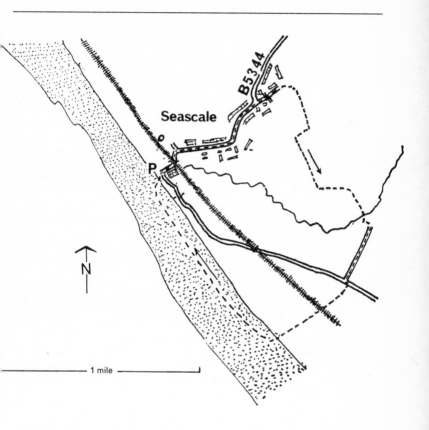

The devotees of Seascale will tell you that it has everything — a fine beach, an exceptional golf course and a spectacular and quiet part of the Lake District on its doorstep. The presence of the Atomic Energy Authority's establishment two miles or so up the beach has not spoilt the village at all. In fact, it has given it a new lease of life. It is one of the places, rare nowadays, where people in the streets bid you good day and the shopkeepers actually smile and try to be helpful.

This is a short low-level walk finishing on the beach. It is a walk that the family can do while mother does the shopping. It starts at the beach car park. Drive down through the village and under the narrow railway bridge (cunningly mirrored) and the car park is soon reached.

Walk up again under the railway bridge and through the village for a quarter of a mile until you come to a Y junction. Hallsenna Road is on the right; take this. Nothing attractive about a housing estate but you soon leave it. Walk to the end to a Y junction and take the right-hand track. There is a view of Wasdale and the Scafells over the gate on the left. Follow the twisty brambly lane onwards. Fell views over on the left include Great Gable and eventually Black Combe can be seen ahead. The lane, now fenced, takes a right-angled turn left through a gate and becomes grassy. When you come to a little beck turn sharp right. It could be wet here. Go on to a gate and through it. Follow the little beck on an unfenced section and cross the footbridge. Turn right. Go through a gate and forward to another gate. Turn right along another fenced lane. (If this section is wet keep to the right.) When you soon reach a surfaced portion of the lane continue on. A lane joins the one you are on, from the farm, left. Continue on.

Join the road at a T junction, turn left, and almost immediately afterwards turn right by the postbox. Go over the railway bridge, on through a dull section to a gate and on to a track fenced on the right-hand side. Go down to the beach. Turn right. The tide line is littered with flotsam but the sand offers pleasant walking if the tide is well out. Your starting point is a mile on.

**4½ miles [7 km]**

O.S. 1:50,000 Sheet No. 89

---

Most of the walkers in Wasdale make for the head of the valley or the lake shore. The lower valley — Nether Wasdale — is largely unwalked yet it has a lot to offer. This walk described goes through the valley fields from the hamlet of Strands before climbing the slopes of Nether Wasdale common which offer pleasant views. Some of the walk can be wet after rain.

Park in the hamlet of Strands. This is four miles to the east of Gosforth, turning right, as signposted, after three. Approaching from Eskdale Green, and turning right as signposted for Wasdale at Santon Bridge, you go for two miles up this road and the hamlet is along the road to the left. There is a small church in the hamlet, worth a visit as it is a typical dale church — built like a barn. The walk starts here.

Walk past the church towards the farm, but before entering the farmyard turn left through the gate. Go down the track beyond to the fork and go right to follow the wall on the right, and to the right of the wood. Go through a wall gap and forward on the track. Go on to the next fork and bear left there though the path is obscure through scrub. Go ahead, keeping to the right of the wood. You will see a wall ahead. Seventy yards from the wall corner, by the larch wood on the left, there is a stone step-stile. Go over this. Go forward on wettish ground towards the crags of Buckbarrow in the distance. As the ground rises there is a good view of the valley ahead, with the famous screes on the right.

By a wall corner ahead there is a gate. Go through this. Follow the wall on your left, go through the gap and continue following the wall. You go through a gate and then follow a track between walls. You go through a gate and on beyond the farmyard. You pass a cottage and then cross a cattle grid. Go on with the wall to join the road and turn left. There is a larch wood right and Tosh Tarn can be seen below on the left. Shortly there is a track going up from the road on the right. Take this. Cross the bridge, go through the gate and continue up. As you rise, look back and rest to enjoy one of the best views of Wastwater Screes. Forward on the left is a view out to sea across the Ravenglass estuary. As you get higher the views are more extensive and if the day is clear you should see the Isle of Man.

Before reaching Windsor Farm go right, up the bank, with the wall. You should find a faint track. As you round the corner you have

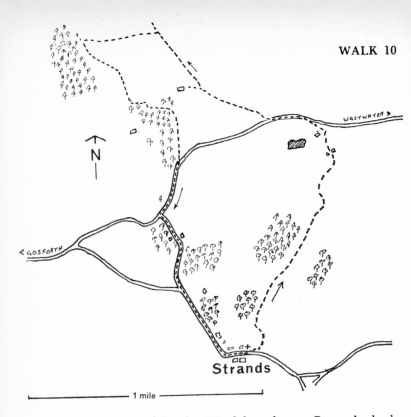

a view over the plains of Nether Wasdale to the sea. Cross a beck, the track levels off and you pass a sheep pen. After this, follow the wall round to the left but keep fairly well out from the wall to avoid the wetness. As the wall bends left further, go ahead towards the corner of the spruce wood in front. This area is now rather trackless but you can avoid the boggy areas with care. Before reaching the wood go round left by a little beck. You are then walking down a pleasant grassed area between walled enclosures with the wood on the right. You eventually cross the beck by the right-hand wall. Go on where the track reaches a ford, go left over it and then down between walls on a sloping track.

When the track emerges from the walls turn right and follow the wall down on the right by a green track. Go through the gate at the bottom of the hill, join the road and turn right. There is a group of yew trees on the right. Presently a branch road can be seen on the left. Go down it past a farm. This by-road is quite narrow so keep a look out for traffic on blind bends. At the road junction turn left. On the left you should see a 'bench mark' which informs you that the height above datum is 261·12 feet. Go past Low Wood Hall and you are back at your starting point at Strands.

44

---

Scenically, this is the best walk in this book. But the conditions have to be right; the fell tops should be clear. Photographers can hardly fail then, and if the lake is calm, the sky blue and there is a touch of snow on the tops, they will probably fall in the lake with excitement.

Wast Water, it is said in some guide books, is sombre and brooding. If you motor in from the Gosforth road by Greendale your first view of Wasdale is across the lake to Wast Water Screes — a great crumbling wall of the fell slipping slowly into the lake as it has been doing since the glacier of the ice age undercut it many thousands of years ago. The screes steal the scene, like a menacing giant. Stand at the lake foot, however, under the screes, looking on up it to the fells of the head, magnificent and remote, and here is something quite beautiful. Comparatively few visitors see this view because they have to walk to it. It is one of the finest screes in Britain.

The walk starts east of Strands village. This starting point is reached by driving down from Gosforth on the Wasdale road and taking a right fork after 3 miles. Drive through the tiny village of Strands, past the maypole erected for Queen Victoria's jubilee by the little dale church, and soon you cross a small bridge over Cinderdale Beck. Bear right and park somewhere on the triangle of land.

To reach this point from Eskdale Green, take the Santon Bridge road and turn right there for Wasdale. After 4½ miles you cross a little hump bridge called Forest Bridge and you are at the triangle of land in the centre of road junctions. Park on the grass.

Walk south as if you were going to Santon Bridge and Eskdale and in a few yards after the hump bridge you will see a lane on the left between walls, gated. Go through here, and follow the lane. There are scots pines on the right and a good view of Wast Water Screes in front. As you walk further on the view over the valley, left, is good. Great Gable occupies the central position of the fells at the head. Follow the track through the farmyard of Easthwaite Farm. Go past the farmhouse, go through the gate or over the stile and continue on down the track. Now you are walking towards the valley head. Go through another gate, and on through another.

Over on the left the harsh-looking crag is Buckbarrow. Go through another gate, and on towards the screes now towering above you. Go

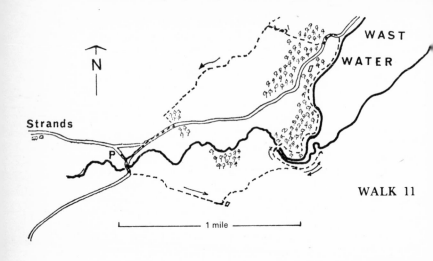

through another gate and cross a beck and you reach a bridge and stile. From this point the way doubles back; but it is worth going on a little further to enjoy a view. Follow the river on your left. The clinkers of an old bloomery (iron smelting place) are to be seen on your left.

There is a good view up the lake now. From this viewpoint Yewbarrow dominates the valley ahead. The building ahead is a pumphouse. This was built to supply water to an ordnance factory during the war; it now provides water for the Atomic Energy Authority's factory and power station at Windscale. The stone for the building was brought from Wasdale Head when the old farm of Down-in-the-Dale was demolished. The pump pushes 2,800 gallons per minute, which does not seem to have much effect on the lake level, and is operated by remote control. Enjoy the view, with the screes towering steeply above, and turn back.

Go back over the stile and almost immediately bear right. Cross a footbridge and stile and continue to follow the river, under some birch and ash trees. You go alongside a meadow with a woodpecker tree close by. Go over another stile and there is an arch-bridge on the right. Cross it and go through the gate then immediately right through a kissing-gate. You are now among some hardwoods, looking splendid in autumn, and walking alongside the river again, but on the other side. As you go further some conifers are mixed with the hardwoods. You come to a boathouse and the path goes left.

Now you have reached the classic view to the valley head, and are walking delightfully on the lake shore. Gable is again the dominant hulk at the valley head so linger here and enjoy it all.

Across to the left is Wasdale Hall, in the ownership of the National Trust and now a youth hostel. Continue on the dry and well-made track. There is a fine scots pine just before the gate. When the path forks go right and along the lake shore (the left-hand way is kept private). Go under a yew tree. From this point there is another excellent and quite different view across the lake to the screes. The wood is a mixture, with some good beech trees.

Go through the kissing-gate and continue on, along the terraced path by the lake shore. Go over a stile and you are walking along-side a meadow on the lake shore. You now see a view of the screes and the head. Boggy ground can be avoided by keeping close to the lake. You presently come to a rough section of path, some steps and a ladder stile. Go over this stile. Climb up the bank opposite for another view up the lake, then go left and join the road.

Turn left down the road, over the grid. Continue on with Wasdale Hall wood now on your left and another on the right, and presently there is a lane on the right between old walls and dikes. Go up here. The wall on the right here is still in good condition. Here was once the hall's kitchen garden. Pass this and continue on the track between walls. Buckbarrow Crag is over on the right. Go through the gate and follow the wall on the right by a path which runs parallel to the wall. This path is only sketchy but it can be seen. You come to a T junction with a path which emerges from a gate on the right and passes alongside a ditch and dike. Turn left here. This is a moss you now walk over and there is a good panorama in view. Go through a rickety gate.

You reach Shepherd's House, a little house on the left. Go through a gate and the track bends left between walls. Join the road and turn right. The dikes here are quite high. After a short while you reach the triangle of land where you started.

**Walk 12**                                    **Head of Wastwater**

**2 ½ miles [4 km]**

O.S. 1:50,000 Sheet No. 89

---

Wasdale (or sometimes Wastdale) has the deepest lake — 258 feet
and its bed below sea level — and the highest rock face in England.
Everyone sees the lake and is suitably awed by its setting in front
of the 2,000 feet wall of Wast Water Screes. Yet the fingers of the
great ice-age glacier which clawed out Wasdale first scratched out
the deep grooves of Mosedale, Styhead and the deep valley occupied
by Lingmell Gill, closing in at Wasdale Head before making the
final scoop. Lingmell Gill rises from an awesome hanging valley
known as Hollow Stones, walled by crags. On its sunless south side is
Scafell Crag itself, larger than London's Post Office Tower or
Blackpool's landmark. These crags have attracted rock climbers
since the beginning of the sport and some of its pioneers lie in the
local graveyard. Only the fell walkers normally see these crags. Yet
given a fine day an ordinary walker with a clear head and well
soled footwear can glimpse them and also get some very fine lake
views. Cameras and binoculars are a 'must'. The walk is a short
one but there is some climbing up a moderate slope and a short
steep descent at one point. You should not be tempted off the
recommended route.

Park at the green at the head of the dale. That is — drive right up
past the lake until a Y junction is reached with a green parking
area in the middle of the Y. Walk back along the road by which
you arrived past a building on the left which was once the local
school. There is a stile by a gate just beyond it. Go over this stile
and on along a green footpath with a good view left of Kir'< Fell
and Great Gable. You are walking towards the fell known as
Lingmell which is over 2,600 feet high although the summit is out
of view. You come to a footbridge. Cross this and come to a wicket
gate. Go through this, turn right immediately and go over an iron
stile. Now go diagonally left, gaining height. There is at first no
distinct path.

The view back from here is up Mosedale towards Black Sail pass.
Forward right is a good view of the lake head. As you breast a rise you
can see the path more clearly as it goes to the right of a tall ash
tree — the tallest tree on the fell side. Going on towards the ash tree
you come to another iron stile. Go over it, and on. By the path side
presently is an old battered rowan tree with a holly growing out of it.
As you gain height again there is a view of the tiny hamlet of

Wasdale Head although the church is hidden behind a screen of yew trees.

Eventually the path starts to turn round the flank towards the ravine holding Lingmell Gill and a path goes down the fell side from here. If you get too nervous of the route beyond this junction, turn back to this point as this path is an 'escape route'.

Go on round the fell corner and you begin to glimpse the crags in the valley head, Scafell Crag being the one on the right. It is sometimes difficult to gauge its height as there are no features about with which to compare it. If there are climbers on the crags your binoculars will help. As you continue, the path begins to lose height. Scafell Pike, the highest point in England, is directly in front of you but again this cannot be seen as it is beyond your horizon. Take care at a point where the path passes a landslip.

This path then joins another one, which comes up the beck side, just before a stile. Do not cross the stile. Turn right sharply down this path as you must descend back to the lake ahead at this point. Take care on the one rough portion, on rock steps. The gill makes a pleasant companion. Its mood varies with the weather for after heavy storms it can rise very quickly, sweeping rocks before it while on a hot day it remains cool and leisurely. The path comes to a stile and gate. Go over the stile and over the footbridge beyond.

Continue down the path at the other side of the gill. The building you come to is the climbing hut known as Brackenclose and is owned by the Fell and Rock Climbing Club of the English Lake District. You reach another bridge and join a stone track. Over on the left you can see an old bridge. This was built by German prisoners of war in World War 1, but floods in 1928 changed the course of the gill, leaving the bridge high and dry. A campsite owned by the National Trust is on the right. You come to another bridge which was also made by German prisoners of war. It was obviously built to last and could not be described as 'jerry built'!

Join the road and turn right. Looking right again up Lingmell Gill you can see the face of Pike Crag to the left of the now hidden Scafell Crag. You eventually come to a barn, all that remains of a farm called Down in the Dale. The disused farmhouse was demolished and its remains taken to the foot of the lake to build a pumphouse to supply water to West Cumberland factories. Just before Down in the Dale you will see a typical Lakeland bridge. Continue on the road and soon you are back at your car.

*Note:* This walk is shown on the same map as Walk 13.

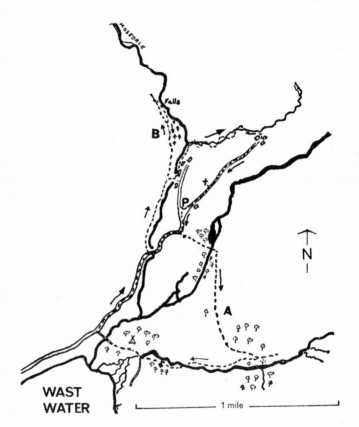

ROSSDALE

Falls

B

P

+

N

A

WAST
WATER

1 mile

**Walk 13**                                   **Around Wasdale Head**

**2 miles or 2¾ miles [3 or 4.5 km]**

O.S. 1:50,000 Sheet No. 89

---

There is a pleasant stroll around Wasdale Head which is not for the
dedicated walker but strictly for those who want to savour the
atmosphere of this old-world settlement. For those who are well shod
and have a head for steep places there is a three-quarter mile
diversion to see Ritson Force, the local waterfall, which is handsome
rather than spectacular.

Park at Wasdale Head on the green where the lane forks. Walk
back towards the lake. Cross the bridge and shortly after this turn
right, just in front of an old gravel pit, and cross the fence on the
right by a stile. There is a good view of Great Gable at the valley
head. Walk forward on a grassy path, which follows Mosedale Beck.
The Black Sail path becomes visible beyond the wall on the left. As
you go on, Kirk Fell's slopes are directly ahead. The path crosses
two little becks and you come to a pack-horse bridge.

It is from this point that the diversion to the waterfalls can be
made. If you wish to do this do not cross the bridge but continue
on leftwards along the path between the dry-stone walls. Go through
a gate and walk on, following the wall on the right. There is a good
view here to Styhead Pass, the main route to Borrowdale, on the
right of Gable. The Scafells are to the right of the path. Notice the
stone-wall patterns. No quarrying was necessary hereabouts to build
the walls for all the stones were cleared from the fields. Follow the
wall beyond the corner and you come to a gate. Go through onto a
path with the wall left and larch trees and the beck to the right.
Two small falls are ahead and they look quite pretty. For the larger
fall, turn right to follow the beck down. You are soon walking above
another fall — go carefully. Follow the beck down, the easier way
being over a little to the right rather than along the steep path by the
fall. Having admired this fall return to the pack-horse bridge by the
route on which you came.

If you did not make the waterfall diversion you will be by the
pack-horse bridge. Cross it and turn left to follow the far bank of
the beck. The path crosses a little beck and begins to rise, then
shortly there is a path down to the right, following a little beck; take
this. The wall on the right looks thick enough to withstand a siege!
In fact, boundary wall building was a good way to clear the fields of
stones. Cross the beck by a little plank bridge. You should be able to
see right to the head of Styhead Pass — the way to Borrowdale — from

here. Cross and recross the beck by three more bridges and go through a gate. Cross another bridge and walk on between stone walls towards the buildings of Burnthwaite Farm. Follow the wall alongside the barn then go through the gate on the right and walk through the farmyard. Join the track, turn right and cross the cattle grid. Notice again the great banks of stones.

You soon come to the little church among the yew trees where memorials in the churchyard record the names of those killed in the early mountain accidents hereabouts. Wasdale Head indeed was one of the greatest activity centres when climbing first became popular early in this century. Inside, the church is an old, simple place of worship, typical of the dales. The beams are said to be made of ships' timbers, gathered from wrecks on the nearby Cumberland coast, one suggestion being that the roof is partly formed from the hull of a Norse ship. Wasdale, anyway, was a Norse settlement and the Norsemen built their churches like up-turned boats.

Rejoin the track and continue on to your starting point.

---

People have lived in Ravenglass for over a score of centuries. Before it silted up it was an important port. The Romans made heavy use of it and built a fort here (Glannaventa) but Ravenglass fort was robbed of stone for local buildings long ago, and scarcely anything can be seen of it. Yet the ruin of the bath-house is surprising — it stands higher than any other Roman remains in England. Ravenglass, which is singular rather than attractive, was once a great smugglers' port handling 'duty-free' spirits from the Isle of Man.

The walk described here goes by the Roman bath-house. It also goes through the grounds of Muncaster Castle which are open to the public for a fee. This is not, however, a dodge to get you in free. Half way round on the wall you can decide whether you wish to pay the entrance fee and wander round the gardens, and enter the castle. Otherwise you must keep to the right of way, and not wander off it by the slightest. No one can challenge your right to walk the route described, or demand money from you for walking it, or hinder you, directly or indirectly. On the other hand, if you step off the right of way you can be asked to leave or pay an entrance fee. My recommendation is that if you have not already visited the gardens, you should walk the route described here, and pay at the entrance gate so that you can wander about the grounds off the right of way, as you will surely be tempted to do anyway. You can then return to Ravenglass on the route described.

Walk sea-wards down the village street to the end. Turn left and go along the pebble beach following the wall. In a short distance you will see a track left beyond a gate, leading up to a railway bridge. Take this. Beyond the railway you enter wooded grounds and join a track. Turn right.

The Roman bath-house is soon seen on the left by a large cypress. How so much has survived so well is something of a mystery for stone-stealers, climbing children and vandals seem to have left it alone, for centuries! It is fervently hoped that its preservation will continue.

Continue on along the track until it forks, then turn left. Bamboos have been planted on the right of the track by a bend. Shortly after this you will see a Y junction in the track ahead. However at the same time you should see a green track leaving, just before it, on the left. Go up this. Among the hardwoods near the path are wild cherries.

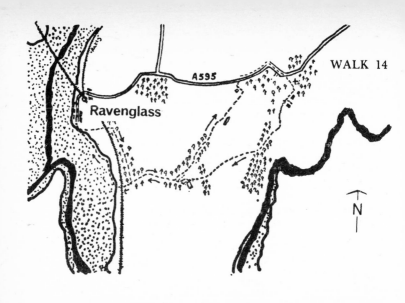

Ravenglass

A595

N

|— 1 mile —|

The path begins to rise, and among the natural hardwoods now are some sweet chestnuts. Further on among the mixed conifers are douglas firs, with light feathery needles, and silver firs. Go through the gate, leaving the wood, and pass an artificial fishpond on the right. Go through a gate, then on to another gate at a walled wood. Immediately you have gone through this turn left. Follow the track past farm buildings and right, through the gate. (You may pass a 'private' notice here which might give the impression that you have been trespassing. Not so.)

Cross the road carefully and, on joining the footpath, turn right. Soon you will see the entrance gates to the castle grounds right. If you have not already done so you must here decide whether you wish to walk freely about the gardens, visit the tearooms and the castle if it is open. If so, enter the gate and buy your ticket. You can then pick up your walk description, after enjoying the grounds, in the paragraph after next.

Continue on along the footpath by the roadside until the path peters out by the school where you will need to cross over and walk along the grass verge for safety. Before you get to the bend cross again to the other verge. There is a climb now. Some distance round the bend there is a postbox on a pole on the right. Alongside it is a track, and there should be a sign which reads 'Muncaster Church'. Go down this lane, past the lodge. The castle nurseries and sales centre are on the right. (No admittance charge at the moment here.) Go on past the church and on by the buildings. A notice may be on a gate here saying 'No Admittance' but this presumably refers to drivers of vehicles. There is a way past the gate on its left and nobody can legally prevent you from continuing. But read the beginning of the next-but-one paragraph carefully. (Ignore next paragraph.) You reach a track Y junction.

If you are rejoining the walk after visiting the grounds orientate yourself by standing at the end of the lane which leads to the church and nursery. This is a Y junction. Stand with your back to the church and follow the directions in the next paragraph.

Just to the right is a duckpond. Move forwards and right towards it then follow the fence upwards over the grass. You then join a hard track. Go over it to join a green path leaving it (slightly to your left) and going upwards at an angle into woodlands. Go up this path and go directly on, ignoring paths which join it.

The path proceeds darkly under exotic trees including bamboos and giant rhododendrons. Now the path forks at a big larch tree. The left-hand path is the more obvious. The right-hand one is less obvious at first but this is the one you must take. It is rather a jungle hereabouts but you should be able to see a path at your feet. A row of bamboos marks the route on the left. Eventually this path bears right and goes up towards a gate in a wall. (Trees are marked here currently with white bands but it is not known whether this is waymarking for the path or foresters' marks.)

Alongside this gate in the wall is a step-stile. Go over this into a meadow. Now there is no clear sign of a path anywhere and the following instructions should be followed. (If you are a by-compass navigator, set your helm to just north of south-west, or to be exact 243 magnetic.) The way is in a straight line. If you look ahead and left, you will see a knoll. Beyond that in the not-too-far distance is a dark spruce wood. You walk to just right of the knoll, towards the point where the wood meets the skyline on the left. If you are on the correct line you will come to a partly-buried large boulder. Move on from this still heading for the point where the wood merges with the skyline on the left. You will be moving on the side of the knoll at its lower level and you should find another boulder similar to the last, used as a sheep scratching-post. Continue on the right side of the knoll now continuing on the same, straight line, heading directly for the wood now. Yet another, but smaller, boulder marks the way. When you reach the wood on this line you *should* find a stile. At the time of writing there is no stile, but the fence is down.

Now a path should be seen faintly going down through the wood although bracken and brambles partly obscure it. Trouble here is that without a stile to mark the exact spot of entry into the wood, walkers have tended to spread themselves and leave no clear line. Going on the right line you should meet a gap in a broken wall. Go through it and go left with the wall and fence until you cross a little beck by a large tree. Turn immediately right and go directly down the field to another large tree. Turn immediately right and go directly down the field to the right of the house which you will soon see. (Keep to the right of the electricity pole.) You should find an old wicket gate in the wall. (Lift to unlatch it.) Go through the gate, and turn right, on the track beyond.

Following this track and round left, ignoring tracks joining it, until you reach a T junction. Turn left. Continue on this track for a short distance and you will see a way under a railway bridge on the right. Go through here and find yourself on the beach. Walk right, along the beach, to the village. In the unlikely coincidence of your reaching this point at a high spring tide, you can walk back the way you came; continuing on however past the junction you will pass the Roman bath-house again to find your way under the railway arch by which you entered.

**6¾ miles [11 km]**

O.S. 1:50,000 Sheet No. 96

---

This is a walk on a mild open fell fanned by sea breezes, and it ends by way of a track in a quiet woodland valley far from hurrying traffic. Probably your only company will be the grouse, curlews, larks and the resident buzzards.

Muncaster Fell is a tongue of land separating the foot of the valleys of Eskdale and Miterdale. The varied walk is highly recommended, though it is so unfrequented that the rule about leaving details of your route with someone, in case of mishaps, should apply. Be prepared to walk on wet ground.

The walk starts near Eskdale Green Station on the 'Ratty' railway. You can either park your car in Eskdale Green (see Walk 17), in which case you walk eastwards towards Eskdale from the village down the road past the Outward Bound School, when you will see the station down the hill on the right, or you could park at Ravenglass and come by 'Ratty' to Eskdale Green Station. The track begins outside the station and runs parallel with the line. This lane is readily seen from the road, past the cottage. If you arrive by train leave the station, do not join the road but turn immediately right.

The lane has a wall left and a hedge right. The track divides at a Y junction, the track on the right crossing the railway line. Continue on, left, still between a wall and hedge and bank. Avoid wetness by going left. The track is rather overgrown in places and there are wet sections. A beck is reached by a right-hand bend and this encroaches on the path. Go forward to the gate and go through it, fording the beck by stepping stones. After passing through the gate move over right towards a wall. Probably the original line of the footpath has been lost in the bad gorse thicket (good for birds, though).

Where the wall curves off right, watch for the wet section and keep left of it and then head back towards the wall. You reach a broken stile and go over it. Keep to the left of wet ground again. The wall goes off to the right and there is a gate. Go through this gate and instead of going with the wall this time carry on ahead on a faint footpath on grass towards a distant wall, going between gorse thickets. Look left at the farm building made of local stone as if it had grown out of the ground. You come to a point where a fence comes from the left to join the wall in front of you. Go through the gate in the fence and turn right immediately, to pass through another gate in the wall. Go right for a few yards following the wall

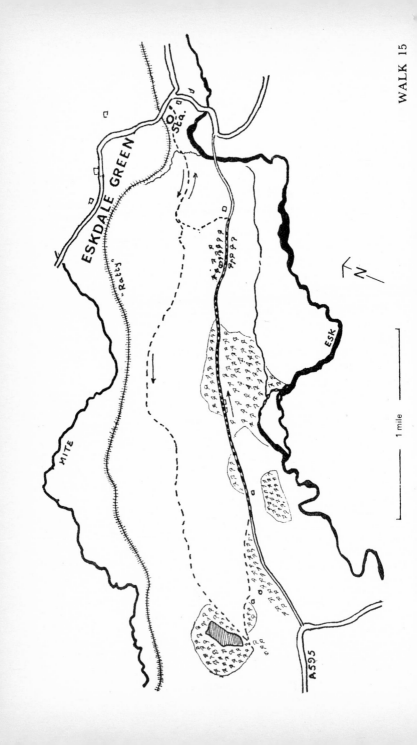

ESKDALE GREEN

MITE

"Ratty"

Sta.

N

ESK

A595

1 mile

WALK 15

on the right. When a corner is neared you should see a path going left up the fell. This is your way. The path bears right after a few yards and climbs, still through gorse bushes.

The path is narrow and it meanders a little, going by wind-shaped oaks. The path then tends to curve off right, crossing a grassy area and you can see off right to Burnmoor to the slopes of Scafell. The village of Eskdale Green is toy-like below. The valley beyond Eskdale is Miterdale, the fell flanking its left is the gentle side of Wastwater Screes. The path curves left a little and there is a wet area and you go through a gateway in a wall. There is a sheepfold on the right. Gymnasts can avoid the water. This area rejoices under the name of Rabbit How. My dog assures me that this is a misnomer. One now has to go forward up the fell, and wet ground is difficult to avoid. There are typical bog plants — bog asphodel, sundew and butterwort — among the mosses while heather grows on the drier patches. There is also cranberry here, though it is a shy plant and not easy to find. You can then strike the more obvious path which goes off to the left.

This path skirts the fellside and gives good views left, over Birker Fell. This was obviously an important track at one time for it was built with some trouble, being cut out of the fellside. As you go along you will notice that stones cleared from the path have been stood up in places alongside it to act as markers. The path rises gently and delightfully. Now there are bilberries. The view down left, too, into the valley of the Esk is quite delightful. The path curves right and levels off a little, crossing a plateau. There is a view then left out to sea over the lower Esk.

The path descends, goes along a causeway, and then curves right. Standing stones are a help. The path gets less distinct as it curves off left, gains height and then goes slightly right. You can see the line of the path, even though it is less distinct. It meanders slightly and then for a time goes parallel with an old wall on the right. There is then a steady climb and the wall side is eventually reached, at a corner. From here it goes right and forward towards a little crag face in front. Note how the surviving trees are the hardy pioneers — mountain ash, birch and sallow. The crag is weather-shattered; an ideal spot for foxes. The way is now more clear and a gate and stile can be seen in a wall ahead. Make for this and go over the stile. Follow the green path beyond the stile. You are on a plateau with good views all round. The path curves off left and begins to climb again.

You then reach a flat stone, on which the date 1883 is carved, standing on some others. This is Ross Camp. Local folk say that the stone marks the spot where shooting parties in the old days stopped for lunch. No one can say who lifted the stone, or how. There is a splendid view over the Cumberland coast. You can also see from the Scafells to Bowfell, the great mass of fell which borders the high east of Eskdale, right round to the great hump on the Cumberland coast which is Black Combe. On a clear day you should see the Isle of Man, too.

The path continues on its airy way with a salt tang in the air. It meanders, dips and rises and standing stones keep marking the way intermittently. Do not attempt to cut corners of zig-zags as you may find yourself bog-bound. The little yellow flower in profusion here is tormentil. At one point another old built-up track can be seen joining from the right. The path eventually runs alongside a fence. There is a view right to Windscale and the Atomic Energy Authority's complex. An ugly power line crosses the scene. Following the fence, which bounds the wood, you come to a made-up road. Go through the kissing-gate. The attractive firs on the right in the wood are noble firs. A tarn can be seen over a gate on the right but this is private land and you may not approach the water.

Now just after this point a green path strikes off left between rhododendrons. Go down here. The path soon curves left alongside a wood, a mixed hardwood. Go through an iron wicket gate and continue alongside the wood. The path is slightly away from the wall but running parallel. There are buildings below including an odd tower, a folly. Continue by the wall side. The path is on a kind of terrace and you go under the power lines again. As the wood finishes on the right there is a little group of californian redwood trees. The track then goes through a gap in the wall and joins a hard-surfaced track at a T junction. Turn left.

Go past some buildings with a row of yew trees which must be older than the buildings. This is High Eskholme. Spruce plantations are now on the left, fields on the right, one of which has been ploughed for planting. Shortly after this a wall can be seen coming in and a ruin by it. Just after this there is the site of a Roman tile kiln on the right. Little can be seen of this site except the notice from the Ministry of Works which in effect is a warning not to disturb the area. Did the Roman road from Hardknott to Ravenglass go this way? Looking at a map this would be an obvious line for the road and a tile kiln would be conveniently sited beside a road.

Now the track rises a little and there are mixed plantings on both sides. After passing more plantings of larch you approach another group of buildings known as Muncaster Head. This is where you turn off this track.

Look left and you will see a track going off through the farmyard. Go through this by the side of the large barn, and forward through the gate. Go on along the track beyond it. The track climbs. There is a well-built wall on the left, coming in from the left. You approach a gate, but just before this there is a gate on the right and this is the one you go through. (You may recognise it.) Incline right to pick up the faint track across the field, past a telephone pole. This goes along the fringe of the field on a sort of natural terrace. You come to a gate again by a wall corner. Pass through it and on. Go through the next gate at the fence. Go right of the oak-crowned knoll, then make left towards the wall. Follow the wall down again under the crab-apple tree. Follow the wall round and you will find yourself back at the ford and walking on the track to Eskdale Green.

**6 miles [9.5 km]**

O.S. 1:50,000 Sheets Nos. 89 and 96

---

If you visit Cosforth the old stone cross in the churchyard should not
be missed: It is dated at about the tenth or eleventh century and is of
Norse origin, bearing a strange mixture of Christian and pagan
carvings.

But at Irton, just over two miles away as the bird flies, is an even
older cross, also almost intact. It is about eleven hundred years old
and was carved at the time when the Anglian people were settled in
the area before the Norse 'invasion'. (It is probable that the Norse
settlement was a peaceful affair as there is evidence that Angles and
Norse lived amicably in the Lake District together.) The cross is
obviously a fine piece of Anglian art and ought really to be in a glass
case. One can motor to the churchyard where it stands, but the walk
described could be regarded as a sort of pilgrimage to a thousand-
year-old relic. The country around Irton is rather flat and unin-
teresting so a woodland section is added for variety. There is a short
section of wet ground.

From Gosforth take the Eskdale road via Santon Bridge. After
crossing the bridge climb half a mile up the hill and park on the wide
grass verge by the sign reading 'Public Bridleway Slapestones'. This
is on the right-hand side just at the forest boundary. From Eskdale
Green it is 2¼ miles and it is on the left at the farthest forest
boundary before descending the steep hill.

Go through the gate and onto a track between the forest fence
left and the wall right. On the left, oaks have been planted — these
are red oaks from North America. There is a muddy section in this
lane so keep well to the right of it. Further down there is a conifer
mixture, then larch. Way over on the right you can see the coast
with the Atomic Energy Authority's cooling towers prominent. Go
through a gate and the track begins to lose height. After wet weather
it could be fairly muddy. As you go further into the wood there is a
varied mixture of conifers. Avoid a muddy section left. A forest road
is reached; cross it and continue on a green track. Silver birches grow
naturally here and some more red oaks have been planted. The track
bears left through an old gateway in a wall. A tarn will be seen
through the birch trees on the left.

The green track joins a forest road. Turn left along this road for
about forty yards only. Look right down what appears to be a
pathless jungle. The right of way goes down here following the little
becks. Step courageously down, making your way down, following

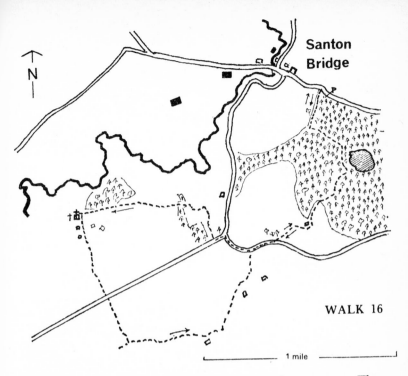

↑ N

Santon
Bridge

WALK 16

1 mile

the running water and avoiding the wetness as best you can. There are spruce plantations left and right, but you are walking among birches and can hardly go wrong. Near the bottom is a low structure which covers a private water supply. Below and right is a gate. Go through this and pass along the track beyond, under the pines. Go through the gate and on towards Parkgate farmhouse. Go through the farmyard and bear right and go through the gate leading onto a hard track. Continue on. The way goes down a dip and then rises. Go through the gate onto the road and turn right.

Go round the bend in the road past the buildings and on to the road junction and here turn left. Irton Hall, seen across the fields on the right is now a special school for spastic children. Shortly the iron fence on the right turns a corner. There is a gate here. Go through this and into the field. There is no sign of a path but a right of way goes on across the field, parallel with the fence of Irton Hall property over on the right. There is a view right up Wasdale, featuring the fells west of the lake, Seatallon being the largest bulk. Continue with the fenced plantation over on the left and the Hall over on the right. Keep to the right of the wet hollow.

Look left for the faint path which bridges this hollow shortly. This is an old way from the Hall to the church and is the right of way.

Go left by the path across this hollow. The church tower should now be seen, in front. Follow the path alongside a fence on the right for a short distance then go through the gateway with the heavy gateposts which mark the end of the Irton Hall park proper. Beyond the gate the track is probably chewed up by cattle but keep as much to the left as you can. Go forward at the end of this lane into another field, keeping now to the right to avoid the boggy section, then going left to follow an old hedge. Looking back right you can now see the head of Wasdale and from left to right Yewbarrow, Kirkfell and Great Gable, and the flank of Lingmell, then the summit section of Wastwater Screes. Go through another gateway.

Now do not go ahead towards the farm. Incline right across the field to pass through a gateway at the corner of the wood. Follow the edge of the wood. The tower of the church will now be seen ahead. The wood, right, is interesting because it is a typical mixed hardwood planting, mainly oak and birch. You come to a ramshackle gate; go through it and on towards the church, along the edge of the field. Go through a decrepit kissing-gate and across the land and through the iron kissing-gate into the churchyard.

The cross is on the far side of the church amongst a little forest of modern gravestones. (The cross in the corner is a modern copy.) The decoration on the cross is typical Anglian work of its period — interlacing and intricate knotwork. On the west face was a runic inscription, now lost. The decoration, which is worthy of close examination, was executed obviously with care and feeling.

Although there has been a place of worship on this land for many centuries there is little of historical note in the church itself though its interior has character. Leave the churchyard by the way you entered, then go right down the track past the vicarage, and pass the school. You reach the road, cross it with care and go down the lane opposite. It is hedged and ornithologists will be watching carefully. Eventually a track crosses this lane and you turn left along it. This is a dirt track also between hedges — a lot of alder and sallow in them as they like damp ditches. Wood End Farm is on the right and after this the track surface is better. You pass a tree-sheltered barn. The track curves below hedgerow trees and there is another farm, called Kitchen Ground, on the right. Continue on past another junction right by two big oak trees and a quarry. You soon come to the road again. Turn right.

Within a quarter of a mile the road curves right and on the left is the gate down to Parkgate Farm again. Go down this, through the farmyard and on along the track by which you arrived, and up by the becks to the forest road near the tarn.

---

Everyone knows of Wasdale and Eskdale. Few visit the dale between the two. It is a lonely hidden dale known only to the lakeland enthusiast. It hides its beauty and has remained unspoilt. A road goes only a part way up the dale. Above its end is a remote and haunting solitude. Yet a glance at a map will explain why it was once better known than now. Ravenglass, at its end, was an important port. The pack-horse route from Keswick to Ravenglass came down the dale and it is said that it once boasted an inn. Activity in the valley declined as traffic was switched to Whitehaven with its growing industry. Now there are only ruins at the valley head.

This is a walk for those seeking a quiet beauty of a kind which is becoming increasingly difficult to find. But it is a wet one. Nobody should attempt it in ordinary low shoes which will most probably get left behind in clinging mud. There are also becks to be forded, though no swimming is necessary.

Park in the village of Eskdale Green on the Gosforth-Ulpha road 5 miles east of Gosforth. Alternatively, park in Ravenglass and travel by 'Ratty', the narrow-gauge railway, to Irton Road station and walk right, to the village centre.

The walk starts at the lane by the Outward Bound School. This is east of the post office and the basket maker's shop. There is a telephone box at the end of this lane. Walk up it between walls of rough granite. They support some shade-bearing plants, and there are quite a few ferns, notably the common polypody.

The track climbs and turns and then there is a green track leaving this track on the right. Go up this. Go through the gate and pick up the green footpath going with a wall, on the left. The peak of Harter Fell can be seen up at the head of Eskdale. The path forks; go left with the wall. Beware of wet ground but continue on the rough ground either to the left or right of it, keeping parallel with the wall. The path becomes a little obscure in bracken and climbs to a shoulder below a weather-shattered crag. Now the wall goes alongside a plantation. Continue to follow it. The Scafell range can be seen ahead and there is a fine view of Miterdale down below on your left. The fell on the other side of Miterdale is Whin Rigg. If you have already marvelled at the grim wall of shattered rock called the Wast Water Screes, from Wasdale, you may be surprised to learn that this is the same fell although it is smooth and rounded on this east side.

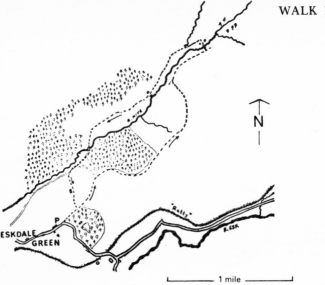

The path curves right and there is another view of Harter Fell ahead. Go through a gate, which opens awkwardly through the fence and the path curves left. Keep close to the edge of the crag on the right to avoid the worst of the bog, then go back to the wall. At the next little crag outcrop go right of it and step onto its small flat summit. This is a fine platform for views and a rest. You can see on to Scafell on the right and left you can see out to sea. If the sky is blue and the curlews are calling you can ask for nothing more.

Keep to the right of the next bog, keeping the wall in sight on the left. Turn sharply left to it beyond the swamp and follow the wall down — take care as it is steep here. At the foot go right to avoid the worst of the swamp, then go to a gate with an awkward fastening, at the wall side. Now you are in a field with no apparent path as probably all traces of it are lost in wet ground and steer-trampled earth. The line of it continues down the field at some distance from the wall and parallel to it. Make for the hard-surfaced track which crosses at the field bottom. Having joined this track turn right. This is the old valley road, now only used by the Forestry Commission.

Go through the gate and continue on the track. There is a larch plantation on the right and you should ignore the gate on the left leading to the building across the river. The track deteriorates. Follow the wall on the left and go through the gate. There is bogland here and you should keep either to the right or left of it. Cross the old bridge but look at it from the other side as it is a fine example of simple country workmanship. How are arches made? A local farmer

66

once told me, with a straight face, 'You get t'biggest man in t'dale, and he stands in t'beck, crouched, with his hands on his knees, an' you build on t'top of his back.' Go on to the ruin of Miterdale Head and into what was once the farmyard.

Leave the old farmyard left between walls as you are now to go down the valley on this side of the river Mite, (hence 'Miterdale'). Keep to the left wall to avoid the worst of the mud. Do not go right on up the hill but go left through the old gateway by a hollow ash tree. Note how one of the iron hangings of a gate, put into the ash trunk, has been grown round. Go on along the track and come to a ford. You will need to cross this and it will give no difficulty unless someone has built a dam along the stepping stones. (If so, and if possible, destroy it.) There is a restored building right called Bakerstead. Go past it and onto a faint path to a wall gap. Go on to the next wall gap and follow the Forestry Commission fence. Go on through gorse bushes and you will soon see meadows over the fence on the right. Bear left to avoid the worst of the mud and go through the gate in the wall. Now follow the old fence on the left. Ford a little beck and go through the gate, through a pen and through another gate. Follow the river side, ford another little beck and go on to Low Place Farm.

Just before reaching the farm note the sign in the wall on the right written by a local humorist in dialect 'Hod reet fr Eshdale', which translated means 'Hold (keep) right for Eskdale'. Following this advice, go through the gate, through the farmyard and on, on a good track. A natural wood of oak, birch, and alders is over on the right, contrasting with the Forestry Commission's plantings. There is a fork, a green track going right, but go left on the hard track to the bridge. You join a macadam road. Go on down it through a gate. Soon there is a track on the left through a gateway. Before joining this take a last look at the river Mite on the right, with another simple bridge over it.

Climb up the lane. Just before the old farmhouse of Low Holme Farm there is a spectacular hollow oak. Go on past the buildings. Note the yew tree right. It was common practice in the old days to plant yews by farmsteads. There is a seat left, with a box alongside it holding religious tracts: an evangelist's novel idea which you may think deserves to prosper. A text is affixed to a nearby rock. The track soon begins to drop downwards; even as sinners fall into iniquity. Then the way should look familiar 'and then ye shall return every man unto his possession' (Deut. 3:20).

5½, 3½ or 2 miles [9, 5.5 or 3 km]

O.S. 1:50,000 Sheets Nos. 89 and 96

---

Stanley Ghyll is a delightful wooded gorge in Eskdale, with a fine waterfall (which can be seen by all, but dramatically at close quarters only by those with good footwear and a head for heights). Three alternatives are offered here: A) A round walk of 5½ miles, marred in its second half by the need to walk alongside, and on, a secondary road. B) A 3½ mile walk using 'Ratty', the narrow-gauge railway, to take you back to the starting point. C) A 2 mile there-and-back walk up the ghyll. Tree books would be useful.

**Route A:**  Park near Forge Bridge, which is east of the village of Eskdale Green. Drive on as if you are going up Eskdale, but continue right after passing the King George. You soon cross a bridge over the Esk and you can park on the verge just beyond. Alternatively you might start from the narrow-gauge railway. Alight at Eskdale Green Station, turn right and you are soon at the King George. The walk starts just over the bridge and goes left upstream and along the river bank. Go through the gate into the wood which is mainly of hardwoods. There used to be a forge near here and the hardwoods would have supplied charcoal for the furnace. When the track forks, keep left by the river. Holly, ash and alder have been coppiced by the river side. The track bends right to cross a beck, then forks again. Take the left green path to the river. Hazel coppice now, with other coppice. Go through a gate. You will see a 'suspension' bridge left. Go right on.

Pass through a gateway. There are now some larches planted left. You come to a gate with a path alongside it through a gateway right. Take this. Go through another gateway by a beech tree with ruins just beyond. You are now among prickly gorse bushes. Watch for a path diving left towards the river. Take stepping stones over the bog. Now you will see broom bushes—like gorse but non-prickly. Picking your way carefully through wet patches, continue by the river to the wall. Go right with the wall to a gate. Turn left through it. You are soon on a stone track under oaks but later you are among cypress trees. You come to a gate by a fine silver fir. Continuing on, watch for the large oaks left and right and then there are western hemlocks planted, and scots pines. At the fork go left. Further on there are hazel clumps with young larches. Go through a gateway. There are now scots pines and silver firs. There is a sweet chestnut left and a

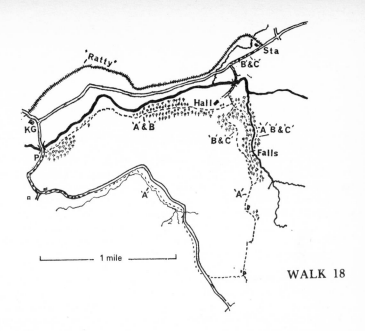

WALK 18

coppiced one further on. Now yet another kind of tree—norway spruce (Christmas trees) among the pines and silver firs. The track dips. Norway spruces left, larches right. Then further mixtures include one or two young douglas firs. A wall is reached and you follow it, right.

You can now see the chimneys of Dalegarth Hall, their round shape typical of the old buildings in this area. Go through a gate. There is a fine mature larch by it and a grizzly old one on a crag beyond. Go on. A younger larch further on has been wind-shaped. Go through a gate onto a stony track going left and right. Turn right. This track soon bends right but go through a gate ahead into the wood. This is Stanley Ghyll Access Area, leased from the Stanley estate by the Lake District National Park and patrolled by its wardens who are only too glad to answer queries. The wood is very mixed again. Douglas firs are just beyond the gate. You can recognise these by their wrinkled trunks. Then there is a mature norway spruce among silver firs.

This was just a woodland garden at one time. Note the rhododendrons—fine if they are in bloom. You are now by the ghyll. In this most shaded atmosphere ferns proliferate—polypody ferns grow right up the tree trunks. Watch for dippers—a dark bird with a white waistcoat and flute-like call which feeds in the water, diving to the bed. You may hear the strident cry of a jay—more often heard than seen as this colourful bird of the crow family is very wary. There are also woodpeckers, wrens, songthrushes, blackbirds and grey wagtails. The place is really a naturalist's dream. Most of the ferns are male ferns, lady ferns (both growing in clumps) and carpets of the more dainty beech fern. Every moist area is covered with various kinds of mosses and darker wetter areas with the flat growths of liverworts. Ground plants include the shamrock-leaved wood sorrel; grasslike yellow flowered cow-wheat; heath bedstraw with tiny white flowers; and in the more open places there is bilberry with small pinkish chinese-lantern type flowers turning into the familiar black berry. Please do not uproot any of these ferns or plants. ('I only taking one' is no excuse. If everyone took one the area would be devastated!)

Go across the bridge with tall larch on the other side. These bridges were put in position by Cumberland County Council — a very excellent job. Continue on the terraced path. Note how the light-seeking trees, particularly larch, have soared upwards in a race for it. Cross the second bridge. Just along the path look right for the moss-covered fall opposite. If you are fortunate to be here when the morning sun catches it, the bright green is fantastic. The third bridge and the area around it makes the only falls viewpoint for the ordinary walker but those with footwear with well-cleated soles, and with heads for heights, can proceed some way further up the path on the left of the ghyll at their own risk. They can see two falls at closer quarters but beyond this the rough path worsens even more. It is necessary anyway to return to the last bridge.

From this last bridge double back the way you have come for a short way then take the branch path left. This soon goes steeply on rough steps and zig-zags, by a little beck. At a T junction turn left over the little stone-slab bridge, and upwards. The path bends right and goes through rhododendrons. It then goes left to an airy viewpoint in pines. *Take great care not to go to the edge of the precipice and keep children and dogs under close control.* Photographers, given clear conditions, can get a fine shot of the Scafells in the distance, nicely framed by the trees. This is a really grand viewpoint. The waterfalls are directly below and if you do not mind heights with care you can approach and peer over the edge and wonder at the great force which broke this granite gorge asunder.

From this viewpoint continue upwards to the stile over the wall. From higher ground just beyond you will see a track ahead. Make for it by the narrow path, taking advantage of the higher, drier ground. Join the track.

(Note: Route B leaves from this point.)

Turn left up this track. Note the rough granite crags on the left, and the farm. Follow the track to a farmhouse. Go left through a gate and down along a track between walls. A track joins from left through a gate, but carry straight on. Note the big stones used to build these dry-stone walls. The track goes to the right of a plantation of pines and norway spruce with odd specimens of sitka spruce with the greyer, prickly needles. Go through a gate and on to another gate by mountain ash trees (rowans), one of which has been used as a gatepost. A track leads to a farm, left. Go through gate and farmyard and through another gate. At the far side turn right on a green path, by a wall for a time, then go directly on across moorland. Join the road and go right. This road leads to your starting point. It is quicker to walk on the road if you take care of traffic but you can scramble down to walk by the beck in the ravine below if you are still agile and have time to spare.

**Route B:**  Start as Route A and continue on by the ghyll, out at the stile at the top, but when you join the track beyond turn right and descend. Go down through a gate. The track zig-zags and as it curves to another gate there is a delightful view up the valley. The pointed peak of Bowfell is way off on the very distant skyline and Hard Knott Pass is nearer on its right, with the walls of the Roman fort just visible on a hillside ledge. Go through a gate and note the lichen growing on the walls, grey, grey-green and orange.

You pass the gate by which you first entered the ghyll access area. Go on along the track past the point where you joined it — in other words in front of the Hall this time. Go through the gate. You then come to a bridge. Note the deep pools ('dubs' local people call them). Walls hereabouts have been badly damaged by foolish people throwing stones from them into the water. Go on past the little war memorial to the road. Turn right and a short way along you will come to the Dalegarth terminal station of the narrow-gauge railway ('Ratty'). If you started the walk by car you will need to entrain and get off at Eskdale Green station, turn right when you join the road and you will soon be at the King George and your starting point by the bridge.

**Route C:** Either get off the train at Dalegarth station, or if you arrive by car, park in the car park here. Join the road, turn right and after a short time turn left by the war memorial. Continue on in the reverse direction to the route described in Route B to the gate into Stanley Ghyll Access Area described in Route A. Follow Route A until you exit by the stile at the top, and join the track. Then go right to follow Route B back.

**Walk 19**

4¼ miles [7 km]

O.S. 1:50,000 Sheet No. 89

---

This is a delightful get-away-from-it-all stroll in scenery which can only be described as pure Lake District. It starts near Dalegarth Hall and goes along both sides of the river Esk to finish at a little, hidden dale church. The bridge at the half-way point is one of those fine arched ones much sought by photographers. The river itself is a great attraction as it slips over granite which varies from pink to grey. The deep pools are blue and green.

The starting point is the car park by Dalegarth station which is the eastern terminus of the narrow-gauge railway line ('Ratty'). You could either drive here or, if you wish, you could take the little train at Ravenglass after parking there and enjoy the rail journey.

There is a picnic area at the western side of the car park. Walk right through this and go through the gap at the end on the left to join the road. Continue on the roadside for a short distance and opposite the old school take a lane, left. Continue on it to cross the bridge but stop to enjoy the first view of the Esk. The land here is private but the landowner allows bathing in the pools. If you are tempted, be warned—the water is usually icy cold! Going further, Dalegarth Hall can be seen over to the right with the great wide chimneys that were favoured by all the very old halls in the Lake District. Go on through the iron gate and then bear left, leaving the hard-surfaced track and taking a track going left through a gate. The track passes into a wood through another gate and you cross a footbridge. Go on through the next gate and follow the track on through fields.

When a wall is reached go right with it and round its corner (ignoring path left). Follow the wall ignoring a track, right. For a short section the track is less distinct but it is soon quite plain again. Go through a wall gap. The track descends to a hollow among lichen-covered blackthorns and the river is closer for a time. Hazels now grow in clumps, no doubt self-sown. The track lies between walls and a farm is approached. This is Low Birker (low birches). Go down left past the farm. Here elm and sycamore have been planted and, where the track approaches the river again, ash.

You now go through a gate and approach Doctor Bridge. The river is again very impressive here as it has carved out deep pot-holes. The bridge is a gem but to photograph it you will probably need to stand in the shallow water at the edge. Turn left at the other side of

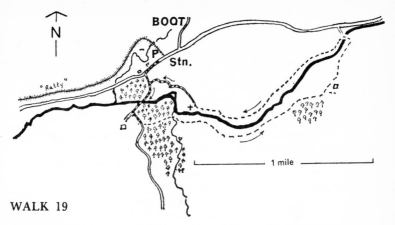

WALK 19

the bridge, go through the gate, and follow the river-side path which is clear all the way. Close the gates.

The only place where you might be tempted to go astray is after the path passes over grass and then through a gate onto rough fell among gorse. There is a path off right here which must be ignored — just go on with the river. Walkers wearing shorts will have nasty things to say about the close-pressing gorse bushes. Those better protected will admire the mass of yellow blooms.

The path eventually arrives, after bending left round a wall corner at the little church of St Catherine's, on its beautiful green river-side sward. The existing church is not old but it stands on the site of a much older church probably built by the Cistercian monks from Furness in the 14th century. Although the newer road alongside the rail-line now passes this church at some distance, its site seems the perfectly normal place for it to be. The whole scene is unbelievably green and peaceful. Look for the grave of Tommy Dobson, the famous huntsman, the headstone of which is carved appropriately with hound and fox.

Leave the church by the walled lane and take the walled path shortly branching to the left. This brings you through a gate onto the Dalegarth Hall lane. Turn right, and right again at the road.

3¼ miles [5 km]

O.S. 1:50,000 Sheet No. 89

---

Of the thousands who motor up the steep and narrow hairpins of the Hard Knott Pass every year very few are aware that they are passing the remains of a Roman fort and that the road follows the route of a Roman road fairly closely. Mediobogdum sits on a step in the steep hillside overlooking Eskdale and no one can visit it without being stirred by its ferocious and dramatic setting among the wild crags. What manner of men were these who could build a substantial military base in such a place? An inscription recently found on some stone fragments suggests that the fourth cohort of Dalmations was responsible for building repairs. They could have come from homes in such an alpine setting. At the time of writing it is possible to motor to a point fairly near to the fort, though there is talk of restrictions on the road at certain times of the year when there are jams and long delays. The narrow hairpins and steep sections cannot deal with heavy traffic.

This walk starts at the foot of the pass, goes up to the fort, so getting the walk's hard work over first. The walk then leaves by the remains of the Roman road down into the valley of Eskdale, crosses the Esk and curves round to the starting point. It is a very pleasant round walk and highly recommended. If you are to spend some time exploring around the fort ruins, waterproof footwear is a must for the ground is extremely spongy.

Drive up Eskdale as far as the motor road goes up the valley. It then turns right to climb Hard Knott Pass. At the foot of the pass you cross a cattle grid and just around here there is parking space.

Leaving the parking point, climb up the right-hand verge and this leads onto a path. There is a waterfall which falls into a little pool in the ravine below on the right. After this the path goes along the road beside a small guard wall, and from this continues on up the grass on the right of the road. The path again joins the road. Continue up the road for a short way to the end of the wall on your left. Now take the green path which leaves this wall corner and goes forward parallel with the road. Shortly there is an abandoned bit of old road zig-zag right, now green and just beyond this the path forks. One path goes right, to the road, the other goes left. Go left. This path climbs and rejoins the road higher. Cross the road and go on the green footpath opposite. This rejoins the road again; cross it again but this time go on the track up the fell side to a little crag, keeping

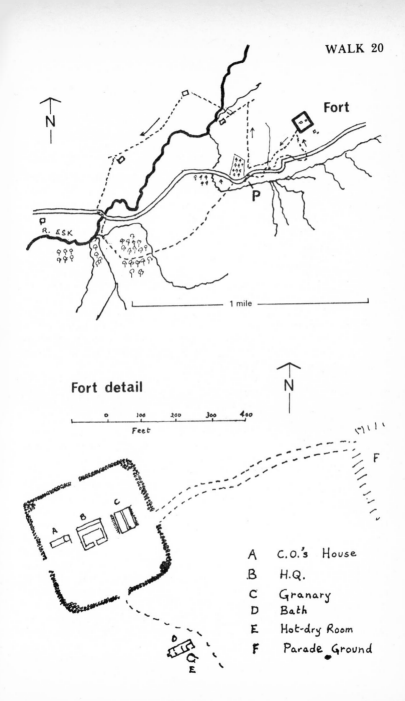

WALK 20

Fort

P

R. ESK

1 mile

Fort detail

N

0    100    200    300    400
        Feet

A    C.O.'s House
B    H.Q.
C    Granary
D    Bath
E    Hot-dry Room
F    Parade Ground

left of a wet area. Go on it towards the walls of the fort. What you are on is probably the old Roman road. It goes round the base of the crag and zig-zags left, then right to enter the fort by the south-west gate.

You are now walking on the Via Principalis. The remains of the first building you come to is a praetorium, the residence of the commanding officer. The 500 other ranks were housed in wooden buildings. Beyond the commandant's house are the remains of the headquarters building, probably a wooden building on stone footings. However, the granary, the next building, would have been entirely of stone. The size is impressive and suggests that it could hold grain enough, if necessary, for months of siege. Turrets stood at each corner of the walls, which were about five feet thick and backed by an earth embankment. Much of the walls have been fixed by the Ministry of Works to prevent further deterioration and facing stones were put back on the wall. This work has been criticised but at least it enables one to see the layout more clearly.

Walk out of the south-east gate, that is on the right from the way you entered the fort. This gate overlooks the road. Follow the old Roman road down over some wetness and you come to the bath-house, a rectangular building in four compartments. The furnace was at the farthest end from the track and the room nearest it, of course, was the caldarium, or hot room. Roman baths were similar to what we now call 'Turkish baths' and this was a hot steam-room. Next to this was the tepidarium, the warm room; and then the cold room; and right at the end, nearest to the track, the cold-water plunge, from which the lucky Romans would emerge refreshed into Hard Knott's invigorating fresh air. Just below the rectangular building of the bath-house is a round building. This was the hot, dry room where the Romans could get a suitable sweat. In view of the conditions which sometimes might prevail on Hard Knott it was probably a good place to treat exposure cases!

Walk back into the fort and look at the setting. It is a remark-able place for a fort. It stands, in fact, by the Roman road which ran from the fort at Ambleside and down Eskdale to the port of Ravenglass. This was part of the tenth Iter and it comes by way of Wrynose to Cockley Beck where it goes left of the present road to join it again before Hard Knott Pass summit, then, coming down towards the fort, from where you stand, left to the present road. Soil-creep, fallen stones, erosion and moss growth have largely obscured the route to all but those with a practised eye.

Walk out of the north-west gate—that is, the one opposite the one leading to the bath-house. Go right a little and forward and you come to a flat look-out point giving a marvellous view up the upper Esk. At the far side of the upper valley is the Scafell range. To the right of this, at the valley head, is Esk Pike, and right again is the pointed peak of Bowfell. A sentry would assuredly have been posted here to keep a watch on the valley, for another ancient track certainly came over Esk Hause from the northern area. In later years this became a pack-horse route and is nowadays used by fell-walkers and shepherds. Forward and a little left from where you stand you come to the edge of the crag, and a huge lump of crag has detached itself from the cliff. One historian has suggested that from this point at the cliff edge the refuse from the fort would have been thrown. It seems the obvious thing.

Walk back into the fort. The only gate which you have not gone through is the one on the north-east. From this gate a road leads to the parade ground, but be warned—the way is now very wet. If you wish to inspect the parade ground leave by the north-east gate. You can see the old road; follow it upwards, skirting the bogs as best you can. The way is less clear as you get a little higher but then you come out onto the man-made plateau which is the parade ground. Here again was a fantastic engineering feat. It must have taken a lot of men, and some very rigid discipline, to cut out this level ground from the fell side and remove all the stones. The dimensions of the parade ground are 150 yards by 100 yards.

Walk back again to the north-east gate. It is this side of the fort which was the most vulnerable to attack. Alas, many of the stones of the fort were taken away to build local farms. It has been recorded that the best-faced stones were taken away by the cartload in the 19th century. Quite a few of these would have had inscriptions.

Now walk back through the fort to leave by the gateway by which you entered. Leave again by the Roman road section round the base of the little crag and follow it round the crag right; the road then bends left again and is difficult to see. Go down on the green path which follows the line of the Roman road. This goes left a little and down to a wall which has been built across the Roman road, obstructing it. According to Roman law the penalty for such an offence would be death. However, this land is in the care of the National Trust and a stile will be seen in the wall, permitting you to continue on the line of the Roman road. Go through an awkward stile. From this point you should see that the Roman road goes forward a short way then bends left to the wall. In fact the wall has been built on the road. Follow the wall down and you may see two loops of road emerging from the wall. Part of the present road has also been built on the Roman road. Go down to the walled wood and from here you will leave the Roman road which becomes obscured by cultivations in the fields below.

When you reach the wall at the woodside turn right to follow the track. Now you are moving forward a few centuries for the track which you are now walking on could well have been made by the monks of Furness Abbey who acquired all this land in upper Eskdale in 1242. The wood, left, is a mixture. At the time of writing some of the trees are being felled and on completion only hardwoods may be left. Down on the left is the farm of Brotherilkeld. Strangely named—keld means 'spring' or well. The track curves left by a gravel pit to join another track. Turn left. From this point if you have a dog put it on a leash before going through the sheep pens. Walk down towards the farm through the gates, closing behind you those gates which were closed when encountered. You then reach the farmyard. There are two gates on the right. Ignore the first one by the building's gable end but go to the second one.

Now from this point there is no right of way through the gate. However this path is 'permissive'. That is, you are permitted to walk it but you have no right so if the farmer here asks you not to, you may not proceed. However, so long as this is understood and you have your dog leashed and look like responsible citizens no one is likely to object. Go through the gate and follow close to the wall down to the river. At the bottom of the wall there is a gate, right. Go through this and you will come to a footbridge. A plaque on it records that it was built in memory of Dick Marsh who was killed in a climbing accident in 1964. An Anglican clergyman, Dick was a well-known mountaineer. Cross the footbridge and go over the stile. Continue on with the wall. Go through the stile at the end and left through Taw House farmyard, and left again through the large gate onto the track. You are again on a right of way from here.

Now follow this track. The craggy fell over on the left is Harter Fell. Go on through an old gateway. A single oak is on the right and just after this the roots of a fallen oak show how they anchor themselves to the rock. After a while a little building can be seen on the left. A short way along your track after this there is a gate on the left. Go through this. The inscription on the right-hand gatepost could not be read by the author but perhaps the reader might decipher? Now incline right and go across the field towards the river. The piles of stones hereabouts are probably just field clearances. Walk round the end of the wall and forward to the gate at the end of the bridge.

Go through the gate, left, and over the bridge. Immediately after the bridge go right, through the gate and forward on a footpath with a hedge, left, and the river on the right. As you go forward the path becomes more distinct and you come to a footbridge (rather shaky at the time of writing but solid). Go forward over the bridge and go over a stile just beyond the holly tree. Then turn left and walk with the wall. Follow the wall right up and round, and go over the stile by the signpost, on the left over this wall. There is a natural wood here of oak, hawthorns, birch and ash. Go left on a narrow path among the trees parallel with the wall. You will find this part of the walk among the trees quite pleasant with the Esk down on the left.

After crossing two becks the wall on the left takes a dive to a lower contour. The path is pleasantly elevated with a good view up upper Eskdale. As this path gains height you can see the walls of Hard Knott Fort again high up on the step of the hillside. Cross another beck and go beyond another holly tree to a wicket gate.

After the gate the path loses height a little and becomes somewhat rougher until it reaches a wall alongside a wood. It then follows the wall and crosses two becks. After this second beck you can either continue along the wall side, which is a fair path, or you can climb steeply up with the beck to join a better one which you can see just above you. (Another monks' path?) Following either of these on you find the way takes a dive to a rough section before reaching the beck (Hard Knott Gill). Cross it and you are back where you started.

O.S. 1:50,000 Sheet No. 96

---

When is a lake not a lake? When one is counting the number of lakes without thought of the scores of mountain tarns, or small lakes termed tarns, Devoke Water is forgotten. Yet it is comparable in size to Rydal Water, or Grasmere. But it is way off the normal tourist track, isolated on a bleak moor. Devoke Water has been described as bleak, bare and grim. Well, so has Wastwater. But its appearance depends upon the day, which needs to be fine, and if possible the heather should be in bloom. The lake, open wide to the sky, has a strange affinity with the moods of the weather.

Although this walk is only 3 miles the going is wet and rough. The round walk therefore takes more time than one would normally imagine. But do not be put off. If you seek freedom and solitude this is for you. There is free access everywhere around the lake and you can linger anywhere.

Devoke Water lies on Birker Fell which separates the foot of Eskdale from Dunnerdale. Going eastwards from Eskdale Green you take the right fork after the inn, a secondary road to Ulpha rising to 800 feet. The starting point for the walk is short of three miles on where a stone track crosses the road and there is a signpost. The arm pointing right reads 'Bridleway to Wabberthwaite'. From Ulpha at the foot of Dunnerdale you take the Eskdale road going left steeply. The cross track described is three miles on. By the left-hand stony lane, coming up from Eskdale, or the right-hand coming up from Ulpha, there is a firm grassy area where one can park. A word of warning—if in rising so high you have entered mist, do not attempt the walk. As the area is exposed it is a good idea to carry a spare sweater in case there is a sudden fall in temperature.

Walk down the lane opposite—the one signposted 'Wabber-thwaite'—but look back before you start as this is a good viewpoint. Over on the distant left are the high fells of the Scafell range, the roof of England. To the right of this is Bowfell, and to the right again the craggy summits of Crinkle Crags on the rim of Langdale. Walk along the track past a gate (which is there to stop cars, not people) with a bog over to the left. Raised parts of the bog are heather covered and there is a sea of heather over to the right.

Devoke Water comes into view, with a single island near the far shore. First impression might be that the water is small in size. This is because there are no trees by which the scale can be measured. The

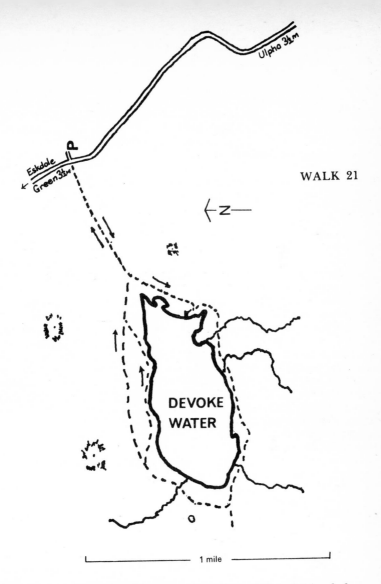

crag on your left has the odd name of Seat How. A little fishing lodge comes into view, and the track you are on curves round towards it.

A green track leaves this track down to the fishing lodge by a large split boulder. Take this. The first section is wet. The green track curves right through a gap in a very old wall to follow the lake shore. A beck is forded and there is another wet section with some poor stepping stones. The path gets faint in parts but this does not really matter; just follow the lake shore. Notice how scrub has grown on the island. The shores would be covered as well but for the activity of grazing animals. Looking back you can still see the Scafell range, the pointed peak of Bowfell and Crinkle Crags making a pretty back-cloth to the scene. As you go on to the far end of the lake, bog is difficult to avoid. Beware of the light-green areas which might be lush grass-mats floating on bogs. It is probably a good idea when in doubt to walk close to the shore. It is still wet but more gravelly.

You cross two little becks and a dampish path is picked up fairly close to the lake. After this you can avoid further wet ground by going on up the higher ground to the left. The track is marked, further on, by two old cairns and another little beck is crossed, followed by another. The way here was marked by two probably ancient, standing stones. One of them has fallen over. Looking back, one can just see that stones, in fact, were at one time laid alongside the track for some distance. There is another wet section with some tricky stepping stones.

Now go on up the knoll in front, making for the high point on the right. From here you can see the sea. A hump of a fell in front is Muncaster Fell. There are a number of cairns in this area which are old hut circles or burial mounds. Looking back over the lake the scene is a wild one. Way off beyond in the fells behind is the summit of Harter Fell at the head of Dunnerdale and Eskdale. To the right of that in the far distance is the Coniston Old Man range. From now on the way is relatively pathless.

Go round to the far side of Devoke Water. If you head for a point to the right of the high fell in front of you you will come to a ravine, the only tricky point of the walk. You may either choose the steep dry way, or the wet easier way. The beck makes a happy little waterfall but this area needs care. Go forward across the heather towards the fell (Water Crag). There are one or two wet sections. It is a good point to remember that heather cannot grow on very wet ground. Steer clear of the light green moss. Left, you can see the works at Windscale (Atomic Energy Authority). Do not go right up the fell, but part-way up you can pick up one of the many 'trods' following lines along the contours parallel with the lake. Do not worry if you cannot find them, however. Just walk on the best ground you can see, at any level. You can now in fact walk along close to the lake shore, though it is very wet in places.

Cairns may be met with whatever route you take. Even though the ground is wet the heather may well be very dry and smokers should beware of the risk of starting fires. As you get to the far end, where you started, the wet ground gets more difficult to avoid. There is a scattering of large stones. You eventually squelch your way back to the track and turn left back to the starting point.

---

No one knows exactly why the old stone circles were erected. They are probably called 'druid circles' but in fact they pre-date the druid period by many centuries although the druids used them later for their own religious and ritual purposes. Scholars can only guess at the earlier religion which compelled its followers to drag huge stones, sometimes for miles, and to erect their enormous bulks vertically in a near-perfect circular form, sometimes with a long avenue leading to it. No one knows either why certain localities were fixed upon. Some of them seem to be in prominent positions which can be seen for miles around. Some are erected in hidden, almost secret places. The Swinside circle is one of the latter. It is a pretty circle and if it had not been off the beaten track it would have been as popular as the Keswick circle. It has to be sought out so its discovery gives one all the more pleasure. The route suggested offers no difficulties except an odd wet patch.

The starting point is from a secondary road leading from the fell road from Bootle to Broughton in Furness. From the A595, Whitehaven to Millom road, a road leads eastwards just north of Bootle signposted 'Broughton. Light Traffic Only'. This road rises high over Bootle Fell and Thwaites Fell and then descends towards Duddon and Broughton. On the descent a road leads off right (southwards) signposted 'Millom'. Drive down this road until you reach a cattle grid. There is parking space on the grass just before this but do not obstruct the gateway. From the southern approaches the narrow road leads from the Millom to Broughton road at Broadgate, 4 miles from Millom and 4½ from Broughton. Drive up this minor road for just over a mile to a cattle grid.

Walk southwards, downhill from Millom, from your car. There is a view over the Duddon estuary with the chimneys of Millom on the right and Barrow shipyards can be seen over the other side of the estuary. There is larch and spruce wood on the right. A very well-built bridge is crossed over Black Beck and Crag Hall is reached. At a junction just after this turn sharp right up the stone track. This area of western Lakeland was extensively settled in Neolithic times and there are hundreds of strangely-placed stones and burial mounds — many yet to be discovered and most of those that have been are uninvestigated. Cross the cattle grid or go through the gate. There is a large lying stone beyond this. Perhaps there was

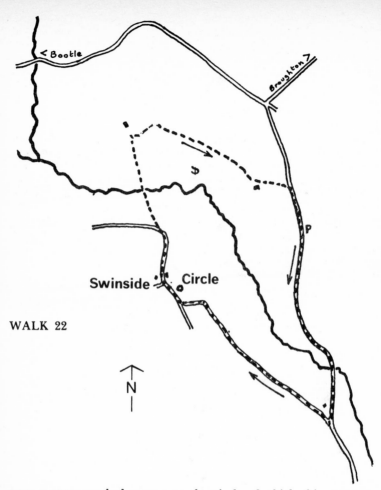

WALK 22

N

once a stone-marked avenue to the circle of which this was one. There are more lying stones beyond the gateway and at least one possible burial mound. Go through the gate. The fell on the left, of course, is Black Combe.

The stone circle comes as a surprise when seen over a wall. The view is a good one—but it should be remembered that if you want to get closer, to take photographs for instance, the circle is on private land and you would need to ask permission from the farm just ahead. The stones are unusually crowded, almost appearing to have been erected on a man-made platform.

There are 55 stones in the circle the diameter of which is 90 feet. Two outlyers on the south-east form an entrance. An excavation in 1961 revealed little.

Go on through the gate and towards the farm. Go round behind the farm to pick up the track beyond. Go through the gate and onwards. There is a mound on the right, and what appears to be an ancient wall. The stone circle is soon hidden from view. The point you are next aiming for is the farm right of forward (northwards). A faint path leaves the track you are walking on at a point where the track bends away left. There is a fence corner near this point, on the left.

Head downwards, then in the direction of the farm. A fence will be reached. Go through the gate and forward, avoiding the wet ground as best you can. You should reach a footbridge over Black Beck. Cross this to a stile on the right. Follow the wall up, go through the wall gap, then go on straight forward and you will see another stile. Climb this and go towards Fenwick Farm but just before it join the track going right. This bends right. Go through the gate. The stone circle now can only just be seen on the right. The track eventually hairpins just before rejoining the road you started from. Turn right for your starting point.

---

From its steep head to its estuary the Duddon valley is just about
perfect. Some of the Lake District valleys crowd all their beauty into
their heads. Not Dunnerdale. The green woods of the lower reaches
are delectable. Travellers going up the Lancashire side of the lower
part of the valley have a glimpse, up on the hill to the left, of a
crumbling castle ruin. It is in view for only a short time, and then it
vanishes, and motorists who drive back up the hills on the
Cumberland side in an effort to find it usually fail. It is in fact no
castle, but Frith Hall, once a hunting lodge and later an inn. In the
18th century, marriages—one must assume run-away ones of the
Gretna Green type—were performed there. It is said a man was
murdered there, too. He is believed to be buried there and his ghost
haunts the ruins. Anyone with a sense of 'atmosphere' will be
strangely moved by the place.

This is an excellent walk through woods and over the hills. There
is one short, eye-popping steepness, but otherwise it is easy all the
way.

The walk starts from the lay-by opposite the gates of Duddon Hall.
Duddon Bridge is a mile west of Broughton in Furness on the Millom
road. Take the road from this that follows the river upwards on the
Cumberland (Millom) side. Duddon Hall gates are on the right
after a mile, and the lay-by is opposite.

Walk up the road (that is, away from Duddon Bridge). Duddon
Hall can be seen through a gap in the trees to the right. On the
left the wood is coppiced—that is, the trees have been felled and
new shoots have grown up from the roots. Presently your way lies to
the right, down a track. There should be a cul-de-sac sign there
and a footpath sign reading 'Public footpath. Mill Bridge and Mill
Brow'. Go down this track, cross the little bridge and go down
towards the houses. Go over another bridge over a beck and pass
through a farmyard and on down the track through the trees. This is
coppice again with a good deal of hazel clumps. There is a pleasant
view over the wall on the right to the other side of the valley.

You presently come to a norway spruce (Christmas tree) plantation
on the left. The track is green and pleasant. After this there are more
hardwoods and then a plantation of cypress trees (which are not
doing well). Then there are beech plantings among the birches left,
and hazels and sycamores right.

WALK 23

N

ULPHA

Frith h.

R. Duddon

P    Duddon h.

Duddon br.

1 mile

A beck with a colourful mixture of pebbles in its bed—granite, Borrowdale volcanic, slate and sandstone—crosses under the track. Just by a gate on the right there is a rock with a wall on the top of it covered in polypody fern. Immediately afterwards the track curves inwards and there is a larch plantation briefly and then hardwoods again. This wood no doubt served the bobbin mill at Ulpha. Another larch planting is reached, left. There are a few Christmas trees (norway spruce). A track comes in from the left but continue on. The track becomes green, levels off, and goes through a gate. The building you soon see on the right is Booth Holme.

Avoid mud by taking to the fringe of the wood. A beck tumbles under the track, beneath a slate culvert. There are birch and hazel thickets with a good deal of honeysuckle. Shortly the river is neared on the right, close to a point where it divides into three. The woodland is then left through a gate beyond a culvert. There is a conical point in front (the pike). A beck side is reached and the track curves left. Go through a gate and continue on by a harder track. Ruins over the field and on the skyline on the left are Frith Hall. A track joins from the left. You are close to what used to be the bobbin mill.

You begin to climb with a deep ravine on the right. Furness fells are over on the left. The high conical fell is Caw; the Coniston Old Man range is behind. The road bends right and levels out. There is a gate on the left which you ignore and then there is a little bridle gate (poor). Go through this. No path is apparent beyond but follow the wall on your left. This goes towards a rocky 'knott'. You are soon walking between a wall left and rock outcrop right with a good view of the Duddon valley on the left. You are walking alongside an open field soon, towards the ruin on the hill. Your progress is barred by a wall. However just before it there is a stone step-stile on the left. (In poor condition, so climb it with care.) Join the track, turn right and go through the gate.

The track goes over a little hump bridge and along a roughish section beyond. The track becomes less distinct but follow the wall. Look back to a pleasant view up the Duddon valley. The ruin of Frith Hall is soon reached, a quiet place commanding a fine view. The ruin is a place of brooding silence now and it is hard to imagine the bustle of the old inn. Like so many ruins it is taken over by elders. You often find elders around old country buildings. They were probably planted for their medicinal properties.

There is a relatively modern barn beyond (private property). Some of the rocks hereabouts show signs of glacial scratches left by the last movement of ice. The whole of the valleys below would have been filled with ice. Continue on along the track and go through an old gateway. A beck is passed on the right and you go through another old gateway onto a pleasant green track with a wall and a fence right. There is a new plantation on the right, and soon there is an older sitka plantation over the wall left. The track is pleasantly heather covered and well drained; a perfect walking surface. After passing a sheepfold left there is open fell, and another planting on the right. The fell is strangely named Penn. It is unusual to find Celtic place names here.

The track begins to lose height. Go through a gate and continue on to join the macadam road. Turn left, go through the gate, and on. Cross Logan Beck Bridge and go along the grass verge. Junipers grow on this open heath on left and right, some quite tall. At the road junction, continue on downwards. Go through the gate by the cattle grid and keep close to the wall on the left with a pine covered ravine left. You soon pass the end of the footpath where you started, and a little below is your car.

2¾ miles [4.5 km]

O.S. 1:50,000 Sheet No. 96

---

Perhaps this walk should be called 'Wonderful Walker', not because
it would be an apt description of the reader if he finished it, but
because the area has associations with one of the Lake District's most
famous parsons, whose nick-name this was.

The walk meanders a little and is strictly for dawdlers. A short
part of it covers the same ground as Walk 25, but the section is
so fine it is worth doing twice.

You start at Hall Dunnerdale. This is a mile and a half north of
Ulpha in Dunnerdale. You cross a bridge here by a three-road
junction. There is a telephone box and a signpost which reads one
way 'Broughton via Broughton Mills', the other way 'Seathwaite,
Wrynose', and the way by which you arrived 'Broughton by Duddon
Valley. Whitehaven'. Park your car on the verge and walk this
latter way for a short distance, then turn right, past the cottages.

You walk on a hard-surfaced lane with the river on the right. Go
over a little hump bridge over a beck and approach a farm with
the typical yew tree. Traditionally, yew trees were always planted by
these local farms. Look at the mixture of stones used to build the
barn here, including red sandstone which must have been carried
from some distance. Oak, hawthorn and birches grow here. The
river is close but the approach to it is something of a scramble
through thicket. If you look at the crag over on the left you may see
buzzards — large birds of prey which are masters of effortless flight.
Further on the hardwoods are more mixed. The river bank, in fact, is
a good example of how plants can live together; it is unlikely that any
of these trees were planted by man.

After a time the road leaves the river for a space and goes between
two walls. Looming up left-front is the bulk of Wallowbarrow Crag
on which you may see rock-climbers. When the wall finishes on the
right there is a pleasant view over green fields. Buildings on the right
are passed and you go through a gate into a farmyard. Go across
the yard, alongside a building on the right and through a little
stile in the wall. Go forward between two walls and then follow the
green path left with the wall.

At the wall corner the path leaves right and is quite clear on the
ground.

Go through a little wicket-gate into the wood, a natural one

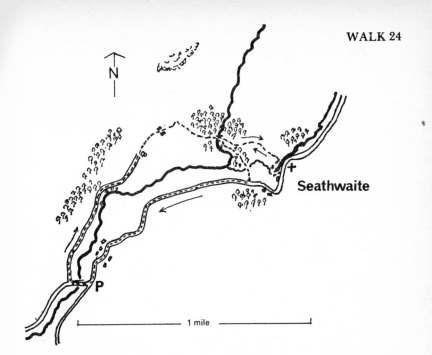

**Seathwaite**

of birch and oak. The impressive crag on the left is of hard Borrowdale volcanic rock. It is called Low Crag — the usual modest misnomer for it soars as high as Blackpool tower from the point where you stand. You are soon surprised by the sight of an elegant arched bridge in the wood. After admiring it, cross it, closing the little wicket-gates behind you. Go forward up the path by the wall with a seat on the left if you want a rest. Follow the little path on across the small slate bridge and among the silver birches. The path is built up on stone where it crosses bog land among sweet-smelling bog-myrtle. The path curves right when it approaches a beck, and crosses an old mill-race. It then follows the beck for a distance and goes across a little footbridge. You then go left along the edge of a little field and through a narrow stile to a road.

Go across to the church opposite. This is Seathwaite church — Wonderful Walker's. He was the curate-in-charge here for 66 years! He died at the age of 92 in 1802 and his grave is forward of the church door on the left. Although the living was only £50 annually, he was able to help the poor from his own scanty stock. He was the soul of thrift. He also taught at the little school and treated the local folks' ailments as best he could. Every spare day he worked in the fields as a farm labourer. He spun his own wool, and he and his wife — who lived until she was 81, dying just before him — made their own clothes. There is a brass plate in Walker's memory, on the wall.

Just to the right of the door is a picture of how the chapel must have looked in Walker's day. The yew tree, of course, is still here, but the building is now much altered.

Now go back down the path as far as the pretty arched bridge. This time do not cross it, but just before it turn left to go on a faint footpath through the wood, parallel with the river. The path wanders through an oak coppice to a T junction. There are stepping stones on the river to the right. Your way lies left, although no doubt children will want to try the stepping stones first. You go through the wood away from the river. You are crossing land in the bend of the river in fact, in attractive open oak wood. Look out for the extra large ants — so large that they make their own paths. The path you take becomes more plain as you progress, and meanders. Do not be tempted to leave the wood at the faint junction but continue right, through the wood. The path falls towards a beck then bends left and crosses a little footbridge which does not look safe, but is reasonable. The path turns right and crosses another little foot-bridge. You then bend right to follow a wall for a short way. Do not be tempted up to the wicket-gate but go on with the beck, and then bend left up towards the wall corner where there is a signpost and a rather nasty stile.

You join the road under a horse-chestnut tree. Turn right, past a lone scots pine and a barn on the left. Notice characteristic hard crag outcrops on left and right as you go along. Some bear glacial scratches, left when the ice age carved this valley out. The road goes through what was once a farmyard, by some cottages and a nice eight-foot high dry-stone wall left. Notice the two lines of 'throughs' that go right through the wall to lock it together.

You are then soon back at the starting point.

---

Dunnerdale Head describes the walk although there is no such place marked on the map. The valley of the Duddon is very beautiful and this walk, which is one of the author's favourite valley walks, has everything. It starts in woodland, emerges on fell-land, descends to the river, then finishes on quiet farm fields. The mileage is difficult to measure; but assuming that you will have some distance to travel to the starting point, you will need to carry a pack lunch or tea and allow plenty of time.

The walk starts at the car park made by the Forestry Commission just north of Birks Bridge which is 8 miles up valley from the Duddon Bridge, 5 miles up from Ulpha. The car park is below the road on the left, close to a rather ugly concrete bridge. Approaching from the Cockley Beck end (that is the road junction between Hard Knott and Wrynose) it is 1½ miles down valley.

Having parked, go over the concrete bridge, through the gate, and along the track into the wood. The first trees are spruce and pines. Ignore the track off right. There is presently a larch plantation to the right. As you gain height there are views left. The large fell immediately left with the odd name of Grey Friar, is a 2,536 feet spur of the Coniston Old Man range. To the right of this and farther away is a summit with a pointed peak; this is the 'gentle' side of Dow Crag, which falls away on the other, hidden side to precipice much frequented by climbers. Farther on, the main planting is sitka spruce. Continue on along the track. The wood finishes at one point. Go through a gate, over a culvert. A track joins from the left but continue on upwards.

The farm on the left is Birks Farm. The crags up on the right somehow combine drama with great beauty and character. This is part of Buck Crag and you are walking on the side of Harter Fell. The wood is the foresters' favourite mixture of sitka and larch. As you gain height, look back and you will see the pointed peak of Bowfell; Crinkle Crags are to the right of this. After the level section the track begins to fall and curves right, then right again, and then there is a level clearing — a loading bay by the track side. At this point there is a track going off sharply downhill on the left. Go down this track.

Step over a little stream and continue on. Ford another little beck and go through a gate. You reach a larger beck now which can

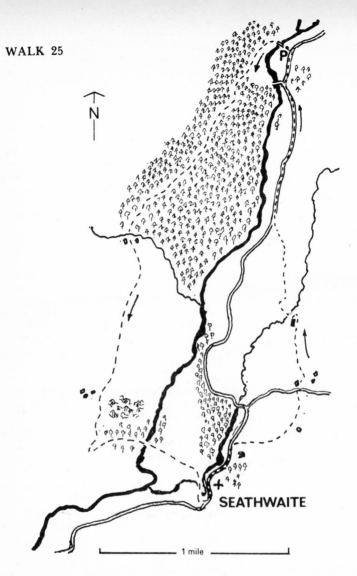

N

SEATHWAITE

|———— 1 mile ————|

be crossed by the stepping stones just up it to the right. Go through the gate and left round the barn over the cobbles. This is Grassguards. Go across the yard and along the track between the walls. This track leads onto a green track with a wall right and a fence left. Pass through a gate and the wall is left and a fence right.

You go by some old ruins and through a gateway. There is a good view over on the left. The track bends right and begins to climb a little. Go through another gateway and the track turns left. Now look at these walls. The one on the right is built with very large stones but all turned and fitted carefully together. The one on the left is made with smaller material but is very neat indeed. The author stops here and pays quiet homage to the crafsmen who put these walls together as this is some of the best work in the Lake District. Some of the stones on the right must weigh several hundredweight, yet they have been placed with great care. Some of the stone is covered in lovely green lichen. Go through a gateway. Just as the wall on the right bends at a corner, an old stile in it can be seen. It is worth just climbing this stile to admire another wall beyond which goes up the fell side on the left. It is a marvellous, unbelievable piece of craftsmanship.

The track then runs onto open fell. It becomes a little obscure where it crosses wet ground; but beyond this the track is built up beautifully. Ahead on the crag summit there are some strange free-standing rocks looking like huge bulls ready to charge down. Go through the gate or over the stile. We leave the bracken area and here, where soil is thinner on the crags, heather comes into its own. The track descends towards a farmhouse and there are some fine walls here too. Just before Low Stonythwaite Farm the track divides. The path to the farm goes over a little slate bridge; but your way is left through a gateway underneath a crag and following a wall on the right. This track falls fairly steeply. The crag on the left is a very fierce-looking one. It is called Wallowbarrow and you may see climbers on it. A footpath leaves the track right, but carry on down the track. It sweeps right and a beck is crossed by stepping stones. Then the track sweeps left and continues to descend. Go through the gate and descend towards Wallowbarrow Farm. Go through the gate, go forward towards the farm, turn left and walk alongside the barn and through the little stile. Walk on a raised grassy path with wall, and then fence, on the left. The path curves right and goes through a wall gap into a birch grove.

You are soon surprised by a lovely arched bridge seen through the trees ahead. Go through the little gate onto the bridge. The river looks fine and clear below and is particularly impressive after wet weather. At the other side of the bridge, walk up the path to follow the wall. Go over a little slate bridge, continue with the wall, and then the path meanders among little crag outcrops. Birch, oak and bog myrtle are here, and soon an old mill-race is reached. Cross this by the little bridge and continue right to follow the beck on the footpath. Cross a little slate bridge and then on over a wooden footbridge. The path bends left and then goes through a narrow stile by some snowberry bushes. You are on a road with Seathwaite Church opposite. This was 'Wonderful Walker's' chapel, mentioned by Wordsworth (see Walk 24).

Turn left, and go along the road. There is soon a turning off it to the right, probably signed 'Turner Hall'. Go up this road, and where it turns sharp right a short way along, go right on through the gate. At a T junction turn left and go through a gate and on direct, ignoring the right turn. This is a farm track. At the house go to the left of the buildings and through the gate onto a green track across to a gate near larch trees. Go on on a green footpath with a good view of Harter Fell forward and left. Bear left for a gate before reaching the next house.

Join the road, turn left, and then almost immediately turn sharp right towards Long House. Cross the bridge then turn sharp left down a pleasant green path between walls. Go through a gate and follow the wall down to a corner where there is a stile. Go over this and across a field to a gate. Cross the slate bridge and go through the gate. Go through another gate into the farmyard of Tonge House Farm. Go round the farmhouse, left along the road for a short distance, then cross the footbridge on the right. Just after it turn left, then right to follow a wall by a catwalk. Before reaching the wood go right through a gateway towards the house. Walk in front of the house and over the stile. Follow the wall for a short distance, then bear left up the bank into the wood to follow a narrow path climbing under oaks, then curving left to leave the wood.

The path is now less distinct. The object is to go to the right of the rocky hill ahead. Incline right along the faint path through the bracken. Go right by stones onto a rock outcrop, then forward on a grass path through bracken again. This comes to a stile in a wall. Continue forward in bracken (towards Harter Fell) then on grass. Cross the wet ground by the stepping stones, climb over a rock shoulder, then bear left a little to descend. Follow the path on to an outcrop, then right to descend slightly on a pleasant airy path. Go over another shoulder then on forward to descend to the road near a cattle grid. Go on the road right, over the grid by Troutal Farmhouse. Then when the road goes close by the river, join the narrow riverside path. This goes by rock steps and comes out at Birks Bridge.

Birks Bridge is much photographed. The bridge itself is pretty, but the gorge below, carved into smooth shapes by pounding pebbles and swept by blue, and sometimes green-looking clear water, is the attraction. The water level rises very rapidly after rain and the bridge has been damaged several times by flood, hence the flow-through holes in the parapet. Your car is not now far away and if you have time in hand you may wish to linger here.

Walk a little further on and the car park is on the left.

---

Broughton in Furness probably looks the same as it did a century ago. It is very luckily too small for supermarkets and large macadam car parks and has escaped the march of progress which strives hard to make one human settlement look exactly like the next. A plaque on the market hall wall facing the square proudly announces that the square was designed by a London architect, no less, in 1766. The clock dates from then, too, and the bell in the little tower above still hammers out the hours. An obelisk in the square stands in memory of one John Gilpin, who generously gave the land for the market. Its steps are suitably worn, no doubt by sitters as much as walkers. Stone slabs for selling fish (and meat?) are still there. Alas the market bustle has gone. The square is a place of ghosts — but friendly ones.

After rain this is probably a walk for wellington boots, and at the time of writing a machete would be a useful tool to carry. Otherwise the walk through the old park of Broughton Tower is pleasantly different.

Broughton is on the Millom to Ulverston and Barrow road, the A595. It is about 7 miles east of Millom.

The walk starts from the north-east corner of the market square. That is, standing with your back to the market hall, the far right-hand corner. If in doubt, of course, you could take your direction from the weathervane. Go up the street there, and there is a street right, a lane left. Take the lane which goes right on. Very shortly this lane turns but you must go right on through the kissing-gate and on along the grass path past the children's playground. Wild broom grows about here. Go through the stone stile. This type of stile is known in the area as 'fat man's agony'. Some readers may painfully find out why. Go along a terrace flanked by cypress trees. Go through the little iron 'round-about' gate, and the path goes forward alongside the wall. Broughton Tower can be seen on the left. It is a modern house but it stands on the site of the old castle. Here the ancient family of the Broughtons lived from pre-Norman times for several centuries. The path runs along one of the old castle terraces, then the wall bends left. But your way is straight on.

At first there is no clear path, but what appears to be a mixture of several. Continue on in a straight line towards the lower ground to the right of the hillock. A path will then be picked up   The

97

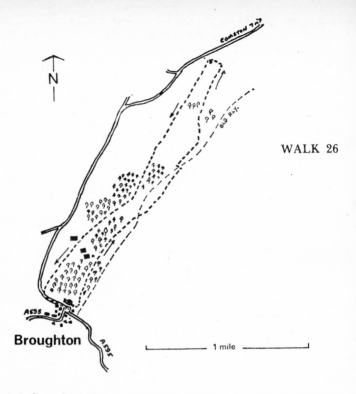

**Broughton**

|— 1 mile —|

landowner has planted some ornamental trees along the path side. Soon there is a thicket on the right — sallow bushes covering a wet area which was probably once a fishpond. Go through an iron kissing-gate under some scots pines. Go forward for a short distance parallel with the fence line on the crag to the left. The path is indistinct but you must now go down to the right to a stile in the wall. You will probably see the notice behind it first. At closer scrutiny this old concrete notice reads 'Beware of Trains. Stop. Look. Listen.' Stop, look and listen for a long time if you want to meet a train for the line which ran from Foxfield to Coniston was quick to receive the post-war axe. Mourn its passing, for it was a splendid route through fine scenery; part of the old Furness Railway's network.

Go over the stile, across the old line and over the stile on the other side. Turn left and walk parallel with the railway line for a short while, go through a gate, now incline right to the hedge and fence below on an obscure path and you will find another 'fat man's agony'. Squeeze through this and go left to follow the fence. After a while there is a gate. Go through it to pick up a track between two hedges. There is a wet section which is difficult to avoid. At a

98

T junction turn left under the remains of a railway bridge. On the right-hand wall a scots pine has taken root. Nature soon takes over when allowed to do so. Go right with the track past a water-trough and a very muddy section. Go on through an old gate and on up a lane which is hedged on both sides.

A gate is reached, right, but continue on up the grassy track between two walls. This was overgrown somewhat at the time of writing. There are pleasant views over the woodland valley to the right. There is a wet section and a shallow ford. Then the path leaves the two walls and goes on through a gate. It continues over grass to the left of a wall. It leaves the wall slightly to follow the line of an old hedge. Go through a gate and another wet section. A gate is soon reached by the road side. Do not go through it but turn left sharply along a grassy track towards the old school. There is a view across the sands of the Duddon estuary. Go past the school building and on through a stile (designed for children?). Continue along the wall side to another stile. You then go alongside a wood on the left. The path is here obscure, but if you go forward you come to a wall. Left of the wall corner by some yards there is an old stile (not a good one). Now follow the hedge wall and fence on your right, all the way. Eventually you reach another stile which brings you onto a path with the hedge on your left. Follow the hedge.

Eventually you reach a wood, entering it by another iron 'round-about' gate. This is a larch and spruce plantation with douglas firs further on. Go through the stile and forward. You are on a grassy track with a plantation on the right. There is a broadleaf wood on the left. Go through a gateway with a view of Black Combe ahead. The plantation is a mixture of pines, firs and cypresses. Go through a stile alongside a gate and forward with a fence on the left. Continue straight on, ignoring the decorative stile on the left. Broughton Tower can again be seen on the left, at the hill foot. But do not go through the gate; go over another decorative stile. (Decorative but very practical; the local blacksmith must have prided himself on this little masterpiece.) Go left to the left-hand side of the pond in front. In fact, follow the fence line and you will reach a terraced path which contours the hill side. Walk along this under oak trees. Presently a wall is reached and at this point move down the hill side to the road. Go through the wicket-gate at the bottom and turn left on the road, walking on the outside of the bend where you can be seen. You are soon in the old grey village again.

O.S. 1:50,000 Sheet No. 96

---

North-West of Broughton in Furness (for details of which see previous walk) is a gentle valley. Through the middle of it flow the narrow pretty waters of the river Lickle. It should therefore perhaps be called 'Lickledale' but no such name appears on the map. In this valley lies the little village of Broughton Mills, usually by-passed by tourists. It is unspoilt—in fact one can imagine that little has happened to change its appearance in two hundred years.

This is a walk from Broughton to Broughton Mills along both banks of the river Lickle. It is a walk that can be very wet and muddy in places. Except after wet weather the worst can be avoided by the more athletic walkers, but you need to face getting your feet wet otherwise, or wearing comfortable waterproofs (not tight!). The walk has another distinction—it has more stiles and gates than any other in this book. Some of the stiles are awkward, but there is none which should deter any but the decrepit. Females may need the assistance of a reassuring strong arm.

It may be well to mention that if any stile on a right of way is obstructed, the walker has a right to remove the obstruction or use a nearby gate, but he has only the right to remove enough of the obstruction to allow comfortable passage. On the other hand, common sense should suggest that if a piece of wood, for instance, is pushed into a stile by a farmer he most probably has an awkward sheep or two which have solved the stile problem. It is an easy matter, sometimes, to take out the wood, pass through, and replace it. Insisting on the letter of the law causes ill-will. Then another reminder about gates: the author happens to know that in two successive years ramblers have left gates open in this valley and caused great trouble. The rule is always if you open a gate in passage, you *must* close it behind you. Dogs must be under control.

Park in Broughton in Furness square (see previous walk), glancing for your direction at the weathercock and leave by the road on the west side (signposted Coniston and Torver). After the road bends right there is a wicket gate on the right (signposted). Go through this and forward on a path which contours a hill side, Broughton Tower Park—not a public park but you are on a right-of-way through it.

The path goes to the right of a little fishpond then reaches a prettily-designed iron stile. Go over it and turn left. The track you are on goes left to iron gates but leave the track before it bends

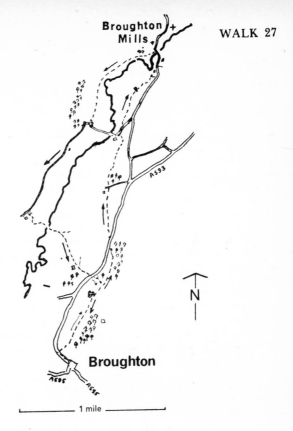

towards them, taking a grassy path below the wood on the right and moving towards the wall on the road side ahead. After reaching a stile, cross the road with care to an opposite stile (signposted).

Go forward and slightly right and continue without losing height. On coming to another stile go through it. Going across the field and bearing left you will presently see your next stile. (If this field is ploughed there is no hardship involved in walking round its edge, though you have a right to press right on.) The stile is of the type locally known as 'fat man's agony'; well-nourished walkers will appreciate why. Go right forward across the field to the next stile. Follow the hedge. Go right forward on the same level and you come to your next stile over a fence. Cross the lane and cross over the next stile, opposite, by the beck. (This is one for gymnasts.)

Go across the bridge and round with the fence. There is a pleasant view over the green valley left and a mixed wood of pine and hardwoods on the right. Go over a good stile over a fence. The path goes downhill, there is wet ground which you might avoid

101

left, and you reach a poor stile. Go forward, parallel with the hedge, to the next stile. Go down with fence and wall, pass through a wall gap near a large ash tree and bear right. As you round the contour you will see a broken old ash tree ahead with a stile alongside. This leads on to a very wet path between walls. It bends left and you follow it, but before it descends there is a gate on the right. Go through this and forward to a stile by the road side. Go onto the road and turn right. As the road bends there is a wicket-gate on the left at the end of an iron fence (signpost). Go through this.

Go on following the line of an old wall. There is a pleasant view left again over the valley dotted with white-washed farms. Take care over the next stile, which is soon reached, if the stone is wet. In fact, take care on all wet stone if you are wearing rubbers. Go over the stile and forward, without losing height, on a grassy terrace-path, then by a hedge. You reach the next stile over a very wet patch. Go forward across a geld to the next stile and a footbridge. Go on to the next stile at a wall corner and follow the wall. Now the path goes through a gate and, very strangely, goes through an archway in a barn. (Mind your head on the oak beams; they are rather hard.) You now go through a secluded and picturesque farmyard. Go through the gate and down the track between walls, then on to a gate. Carry on round the left-hand side of the knoll. Pass through the gate and right, past the house. Go through another gate and through the group of buildings to the road.

You are now in Broughton Mills. Turn left down the road where you will find an 18th century inn, the Blacksmith's Arms, on the left. There is an old horse-mounting block at the corner. Go down past the old mill (converted) and over the village bridge called Shop Bridge. The best view of it can be had by turning right at the far end and going along the road a little. Under the arch you will see evidence that the bridge was widened at one time. The first bridge would probably have been just a pack-horse bridge. Activity at the quarries above may have caused it to be widened to cart-width.

Re-commence the walk at the far side of the bridge. There is a stile on the left (signpost). Go through it and follow the river side. Pass over an awkward stile and over slippery rock to another stile. Then, taking care through blackthorns, carry on bearing slightly right. (If this field is ploughed, walk round the edge.) Go through a stile and on to a wall gap and then go on with the wall and river directly on your left. When you reach a cross-wall there is a very awkward wooden stile on your left. This brings you down directly to the river side where the waters tumble over a series of little falls, a fine sight after heavy rain. There are glacial boulders about the field here left when the ice melted. The path then crosses a ford. Whether you cross it dry depends upon the amount of water and how agile you are. Wellington-shod walkers will seize the opportunity to clean their soles. Go left to a gate.

You are walking alongside the river again and you reach a high stile after which you walk in the open along a green track. Go over another high stile alongside a gate (or cowardly through the gate) and find yourself on a macadam lane. Turn right to a small hamlet, Croglinhurst. The lane crooks right, then left. At a Y junction turn left. There is a high wall on the left covered in ivy and polypody fern. The road climbs and the best view now is over one's left shoulder. There is soon a ruin on the left, now used as a sheep pen.

Left now is a pretty pattern below of hedges, dikes and walls. Go past Middle Bleansley Farm. Ignore a turning left. Continuing on the road you come to a farm called Lower Bleansley. The road dives left to the farm. Go down and then turn sharp left to follow the track which soon goes right and through a gate onto a muddy section although the worst of this might be avoided by detouring right. The track bears left to give you a view up valley of the Coniston Old Man range and then goes right to cross an arch bridge. Little plants grow between the stones of the bridge, which is best viewed from the far side and on the right.

Go on along the track and you reach two gates. The one on the left is across your track, but go through the one on the right and on across a field. Head towards the gate and you will see a stile to its left. Go through the stile or the gate and go on until you reach another stile and gate. After this go up and left, towards the left of the buildings, and through the gate onto a lane. Go right. Trudge through some muddy sections and you join a macadam lane. Go right on until you reach the Torver-Broughton road. Cross it with care and go through the iron gates of Broughton Tower Park. Follow the track for a short time and you should recognise the path by which you started the walk. Go back over the pretty iron stile, past the pond and back to the wicket gate. Join the road again, keeping on the outside of the bend where the traffic can see you, and you are soon back at the square.

---

This is really a low-level fell walk, wild for the first half with fell views and contouring over the dale of the Lickle with views over farms and forest on the second half. The half-way mark can be very wet after the long rain.

Park on the splendid viewpoint by the road summit between Hall Dunnerdale and Broughton Mills. To find this from Ulpha in Dunnerdale, go up the valley for a mile and a half to where the road crosses the Duddon at Hall Dunnerdale, then instead of continuing up the valley, turn right and drive to the summit of the narrow road. If the gate is closed en route, close it after you. To find the starting point from the Broughton approach, turn left after a mile and a half to go through the little hamlet of Broughton Mills, continuing on along the road past the church and to the summit of the hill. If the gate near the hill summit is closed on your approach, close it after you.

The starting place is a good viewpoint over Dunnerdale. Facing Dunnerdale your path is on the right over the grass. Walk on it to the first fork and bear left, and shortly you go round the side of an ivy-clad crag. At the T junction beyond, turn right. At the next junction turn left onto a good green path with fine views left. The path follows a wall and climbs slightly. There is a shattered crag on the left and then a splendid view over the brow. Harter Fell is near, left of the centre of the view. Nearer still is the fine crag of Wallowbarrow below and across the river. You may see rock-climbers on it.

You now cross a beck. There is a good view beyond this if you want a diversion but the way goes right, up the little valley. The path is at times somewhat faint but keep to the left. In just about three-quarters of a mile the path veers left and crosses another beck. The path now goes on towards a wall and past a natural little rock garden on the crag, left. You must make for the elbow of the wall, to the right. Turn right to a little beck and follow its bank. Cross it where it junctions with another beck, then follow the other bank. After a very short distance the beck bends to the left, but you must go to the right on the higher drier ground to join a path through bracken which curves round about the wall elbow. Jackson Ground Farm is on the left.

Continuing on above the wall, you see a good view over Duddon Sands. When the wall curves left, the path takes a short cut to the

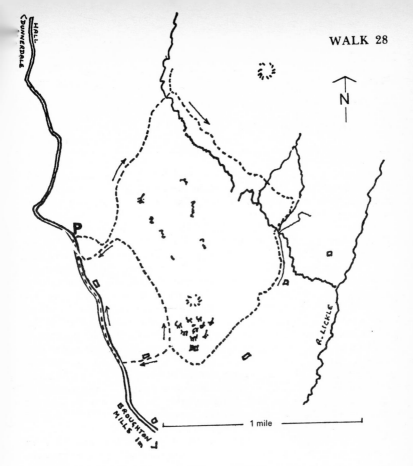

right of a small crag, and you ford a little beck and continue parallel with the wall on a fainter path for a short distance. Then it goes straight on, on the same level. There is a farm down to the right called Carter Ground. Now first the path loses height towards this farm for a short distance, then it goes on again, undulating, and past a large boulder. The path then gradually gets plainer as it climbs upwards for almost half a mile. There is a good panorama left over the dale if you want to enjoy a rest. The path then turns to go through a pretty little pass. Go on and down through the pass. You soon have a choice. Continuing to drop down, you can go through the walled lane to the road, turning right to get to your starting point: or the more intrepid can go right on a faint path through high bracken following the right-hand side of a wall, going on towards the old quarries, but bearing left to avoid them (especially if you have children as there are dangerous holes) to rejoin the road.

105

4¾ **miles [7.5 km]**

O.S. 1:50,000 Sheet No. 96

---

A lot of the old lines of communication in the south-western part of the Lake District were on the sands of Morecambe Bay and the Duddon estuary. At low tides they offered ready-made roads, flat and smooth for horse traffic, and even the speeding stagecoaches. In places, to the uninitiated, they were hazardous, as rivers can change course, quick-sands change position, and the tide comes in very fast. Although these routes are not now used except by the local farmers, and the shrimpers, they are still marked as public roads on the maps. No one should attempt them without a guide, and they are certainly of no use for cars. A short section is offered in this round walk but if the tide is high, or the sand excessively wet, one can walk on the sea-washed turf alongside. There is additional interest for bird-spotters as the sands attract waders, and the cries of oyster-catchers, sandpipers and curlews will be music to their ears. The hedgerows will also provide interest. Bramble jam makers will also have a profitable time in season. As might be expected, some of the going is wet. Otherwise this walk is largely on flat country lanes (rare in a Lake District guide).

Park near Foxfield railway station which is south of Broughton in Furness on the Millom-Barrow road, a through-traffic route. There is a lay-by just on the Broughton side of the Prince of Wales hotel. The hotel has a substantial car park for customers. If the lay-by is full, and you are not an hotel customer, you should find parking space at the lane-end just beyond or in another small car park at the end of a minor road a little way on.

Walk on towards Barrow (south-east), and just before the road turns sharply left there is a level crossing on the right. Go across this and at the Y junction bear left on the macadam road. The chimneys of Millom can be seen right in the distance and Barrow further still to the left. At a T junction turn right. Follow this road as it goes left through a gate. Go through the farmyard and on by the lane. Pass through the gate and onto the sea-washed turf. The pink flower, of course, is thrift.

Now you have a choice of continuing round the shoreline on the turf or walking on the sand which is usually wet. The turf is criss-crossed with channels and dotted with pools. Follow the sheep 'trods'—they have worked out the best way. On the sand route you walk out towards the promontory forward and left. The way goes by

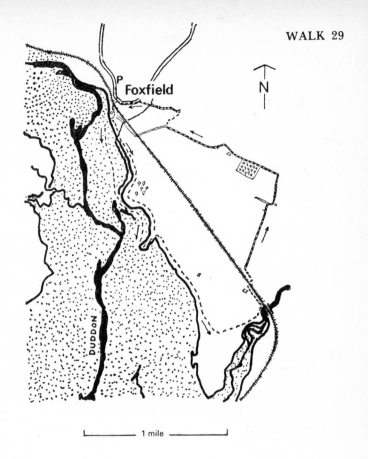

Foxfield

DUDDON

1 mile

its tip. Geologists will be aware that hereabouts a band of limestone, known as the Coniston, starts and makes a narrow belt through Coniston, Tarn Hows, across the head of Windermere and on to Troutbeck, for the most part lying between the silurian slate and the Borrowdale volcanic series.

The promontory is a pleasant place to sit and enjoy the sun (if any) and the bay wind. The rock which has the peculiar name of Whelpshead Crag is covered in pink thrift in season, and painted with yellow lichen.

From here the sands route heads for the end of the next promontory, on the left three-quarters of a mile on. The village of Sand Side can be seen beyond it. (If a mist prevents you from seeing this, needless to say do not attempt it.) If the going gets too wet and sticky you should make for the grassy shore. The turf route continues on as before southwards. Bear left to follow the fence, and follow it round the corner. The large scar of Kirkby Quarries can be seen on the fells.

Now walk up the promontory away from the sands. Make for the railway bridge across the river (Kirkby Pool). At the bridge, just before the line, is a stile, left. Go through it and follow the fence alongside the railway. Go through the stile near a farm and turn right to cross the level crossing. (N.B. At the time of writing this line had not been 'axed' and was a busy one.) Close the gate.

You now join a macadam lane. The hedges are a wild mixture of shrubs and plants; sallow is very common, with rowan and elderberry, there are masses of honeysuckle, wild rose and brambles while the edges are favoured by a variety of wild flowers. At the end of a straight the road turns right (ignore a lane left). Just after this turn left. After another straight the road turns left by a broadleaf wood. Go right of the farmhouse. There is a brief glimpse of an example of environmental pollution — inexcusable when there is a council refuse dump only two miles away. Soon you are walking on a 'moss': flat, wet lands which are attractive to the eye as well as the naturalist. Birch, sallow and gorse enjoy this sort of land, and there is wild iris, masses of heather and bog asphodel which gleams red in autumn.

Now, after the relatively straight section, watch for a grass footpath on the right, just as the road bends left. This is a raised green path on the edge of the moss. Follow it and after a short time it turns left through bracken. Cross a little footbridge made of a large flat slate. Join the track and go left. Botanists would have noted red campion along the way. Left now is bladder campion. At a Y junction bear left and go over the bridge. You soon join the road where you turn left to your starting point.

---

This is a good leg-stretcher rising through woodland to open moor where there are the remains of an ancient British settlement. Excellent views are to be enjoyed on the way and you are unlikely to see many other people. Walking is easy, though forestry operations may have temporarily brought muddy sections. Insect repellent may be necessary in high summer. The walk starts at Causeway End which is 2 miles east of Broughton in Furness on the Barrow road. After a number of bends there is a straight length of road. This is the Causeway—park at the far end in the lay-by by the RAC box.

Causeway End Bridge is interesting, but before examining it there is a warning—*keep very close to the parapet* otherwise you may be mown down by fast-moving traffic. Children must be firmly held. The flat stones along the parapet were carved last century by a post-messenger called Thomas Dawson who had to wait at this bridge to pick up mail. He carved and doodled to pass away the time, probably hiding a chisel among the stonework between visits. Some of the stones may have been lost; certainly a number has been moved during bridge repairs. Some of the inscriptions read as follows and you may be able to find others: 'Happy land', 'Be kind to the poor', 'A sensible man won't offend me, and no other can', 'Yellow for ever' (political?), 'I can paddle my own canoe', 'Shelling green peas', 'England for ever', 'England expects every man this day will do his duty', 'Bonnets of blue', 'Do not stop long at the fair', 'They laugh best who laugh last', 'Nil desperandum'. 'Put your shoulder to the wheel is a motto for every man'. This is the work of a craftsman; the graffiti of yesterday certainly had style. There used to be a date, but on the last visit the author failed to find it.

At the far end of the bridge, go left down the lane towards the wood. At the end of the group of buildings there is a gate before a track leading up into the wood. Go through this gate and on up the track. Shortly, on the right, there is a green track but ignore this and continue on. Now comes a mixture of pines and sitka spruces, beeches are here and there with oaks, and then there are larch trees on the left. Higher, by the track side there is some broom and gorse. Both carry the same type of pea-like yellow flowers but the gorse is very prickly and the broom is not.

The track again branches. This time two green tracks leave the track you are on, both on your right. Take the first one—that is,

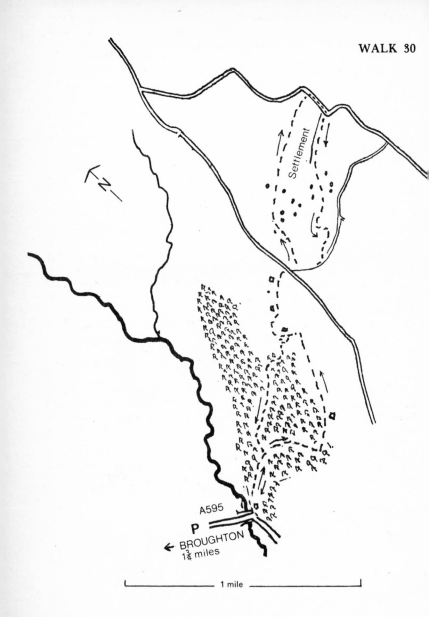

Settlement

N

A595

P

← BROUGHTON
  1¾ miles

1 mile

the middle of the three ways. You walk among Lawson's cypress trees and there is a green path, right, off your track which you should ignore. Unless the trees have grown up when you read this there should be views right across Duddon sands, and to the right of them the hump of Black Combe. Going through larches you begin to reach the edge of the wood and then come among some grand firs and an old farmhouse on the right, Well Wood Farm. Just after the buildings look at the wall on the right for a rather poor stone step stile. Go over and down it and turn left to go through, or squeeze by, the gate. You are then on a green track between stone walls.

Over your right shoulder there are views over the Duddon estuary. The track is a very pleasant one, and shortly you come to an open area. Continue on in the same direction and you will find a continuation of the lane between stone walls. You have an excellent view of Coniston Old Man mountain range, the summit (2,635 feet) being on the tip of the rounded hump. The sharper peak on the left is the top of Dow Crag (2,535 feet). There are fine views all round.

The lane now descends a rock section and you enter the yard of a disused farmhouse. Go right on through the yard and through the gate beyond the buildings. Presently there is a gate on the right to go through. Go through another gate, on through the farmyard of Hill Farm and through the next gate. Go on the track still with fine views and through another gate onto a macadam lane; bear right and you will come to a crossroads. Go right across the crossroads, up the road opposite and very shortly there is a green footpath left and starting from the same point (signposted 'Woodland Road 1 m') an easily-seen green track leading up the fell. This is the way.

The track climbs and curves left and the views over to Black Combe open up, and then there is a better view of Coniston Old Man. The pattern of the valley floor with the varied shades of green from fields, woods and bracken, is also a pleasant eye-feast. As you go higher the views broaden but watch out nearer at hand for the old cairns, some of which are probably ancient burial mounds, others the collapsed walls of old huts. A lot of them are buried in the bracken.

The green track gets a little narrower and there are bigger cairns. The path reaches a macadam road; turn right and go up it, up the hill. The road bends left soon, and there is a green track right on which you should see a distant notice. There is a large cairn on the right. Go up the green track. Cars are sometimes driven up here but it is an offence to drive more than 15 yards from the road. The notice reads 'This ancient settlement is protected as a monument of national importance under the Ancient Monuments Act. Ministry of Public Buildings and Works.' Walk right on. There are odd mounds here and there and on the right, half hidden in the bracken, is the line of a very old wall—the wall that surrounded this 3,000-year-old settlement. Continue on, ignoring a path left. You will see evidence of past excavations in places and an old wall can be seen left. Continue on and you will see the remains of a part of the settlement.

After exploring the remains of the settlement go back to the track then go forward by the Ministry of Works iron signpost and you can go on up to the top of the hillock marked with another cairn. From here the ancient Briton would have had an excellent view of the valley below and across the sands to where Millom and Barrow stand now. No doubt in troubled times he could expect to see his colleagues posted on the other high points. Go back towards the settlement then go right, down a track into the hollow. Join the macadam road and turn right. The comparatively new walls here on the left can give an idea of how high the old walls had to be to keep in the stock.

At the bottom of the road you reach crossroads which should look familiar. Go down the lane opposite, which is the one you arrived by, turn left at the Y junction and go through the gate again. Go on through the farm once more and on through the gates to the disused farm with good views to Black Combe on the way. At the disused farm, instead of going up the lane between the walls, turn right through a gate into the field after the building. There is a boggy area in front so go well to the left to by-pass it. At the wall corner to the right there is an old stile, now collapsed. Go through here and forward following the wall through jungle.

After a few yards a green track is joined. This comes in from the left and sweeps on ahead. Go ahead. The track follows a wall for a short time, then joins another track coming in from the right. Carry on, into the wood, upwards then down a dip. There are plantings of pine and larch and older sitka spruce. A track joins from the left, but carry on. A path junction soon should look familiar. Carry right on down. You eventually leave the wood again by the gate, and the road is ahead. Take care in crossing to your car.